D1426786

International Federation of Library Associations and Institutions
Fédération Internationale des Associations de Bibliothécaires et des Bibliothèques
Internationaler Verband der bibliothekarischen Vereine und Institutionen
Международная Федерация Библиотечных Ассоциаций и Учреждений
Federación Internacional de Asociaciones de Bibliotecarios y Bibliotecas

Dans ce document, le genre masculin est utilisé sans
discrimination et dans le seul but d'alléger la lecture

IFLA Publications 79

Section des bibliothèques et centres
documentaires scolaires

Section of School Libraries
and Resource Centres

Ressources pour les bibliothèques
et centres documentaires scolaires

Resourcebook for School Libraries
and Resource Centers

Edité par / Edited by
Paulette Bernhard

Avec la participation de: / With the participation of:

Colette Charrier, Mary Collis, Margarethe Dahlström, Lucie David,
Lin Forrest, Anne M. Galler, Lyn Hay, Teruyo Horikawa,
Niels Jacobsen, Torny Kjekstad, Benoit Létourneau, Inci Önal,
Richard Morin, Alexandra Papazoglou, Robert Roy,
Ramon Salaberria, Marguerite Tremblay, Margaret Tye,
Guylaine Vinet, Glenys Willars, Blanche Woolls

K · G · Saur   München 1997

IFLA Publications
edited by Carol Henry

Recommended catalogue entry:

Ressources pour les bibliothèques et centres documentaires
scolaires = Resourcebook for school libraries and resource centers /
Section des Bibliothèques et Centres Documentaires Scolaires.
[International Federation of Library Associations and Institutions].
Ed. par: Paulette Bernhard.
... – München : Saur, 1997, p. VIII, 148, 21 cm
(IFLA publications ; 79)
ISBN 3-598-21805-2

Die Deutsche Bibliothek – CIP-Einheitsaufnahme

Ressources pour les bibliothèques et centres documentaires
scolaires = Resourcebook for school libraries and resource centers /
Section des Bibliothèques et Centres Documentaires Scolaires.
[International Federation of Library Associations and Institutions].
Ed. par: Paulette Bernhard.
... – München : Saur, 1997
(IFLA publications ; 79)
ISBN 3-598-21805-2

Printed on acid-free paper
The paper used in this publication meets the minimum requirements of American National
Standard for Information Sciences – Permanence of Paper for Printed Library Materials,
ANSI Z39.48.1984.

Printed/Bound by Strauss Offsetdruck GmbH, Mörlenbach

ISBN 3-598-21805-2
ISSN 0344-6891 (IFLA Publications)

REMERCIEMENTS / ACKNOWLEDGEMENTS

Nous tenons à remercier les personnes suivantes
qui ont participé à la production de cet ouvrage :

We would like to thank the following persons
who have participated in the making of this book :

Colette Charrier
Mary Collis
Margarethe Dahlström
Lucie David
Lin Forrest
Anne M. Galler
Lyn Hay
Teruyo Horikawa
Niels Jacobsen
Torny Kjekstad
Benoit Létourneau
Inci Önal,
Richard Morin
Alexandra Papazoglou
Robert Roy
Ramon Salaberria
Marguerite Tremblay
Margaret Tye
Guylaine Vinet
Glenys Willars
Blanche Woolls

et / and : Peter M. Brown for his overall help and patience

Table des matières / Table of Contents

INTRODUCTION

L'ouvrage que vous avez entre les mains est l'aboutissement du travail d'un groupe de personnes persuadées de l'importance de l'apprentissage et de l'enseignement basés sur les ressources et, en conséquence, des bibliothèques et centres documentaires scolaires, ainsi que de celles et ceux qui en sont responsables. Il fait le bilan de l'activité de la Section des bibliothèques scolaires de l'IFLA depuis ses origines, identifie les regroupements professionnels et les principales listes de discussion dans le domaine de la bibliothéconomie scolaire à travers le monde, présente le résultat de plusieurs projets entrepris par la Section depuis 1993 et recense des ressources dans deux secteurs en émergence.

La **première partie** fait le bilan des activités de la Section, y compris les publications et les communications données lors des rencontres publiques.

La **deuxième partie** identifie les associations en bibliothéconomie scolaire ou les sections d'associations plus générales qui s'intéressent à ce domaine à travers le monde, ainsi que les principales listes de discussion destinées aux bibliothécaires et aux enseignants-documentalistes du milieu scolaire

La **troisième partie** émane du projet "Liste de périodiques en bibliothéconomie scolaire" et recense les périodiques et les bulletins en bibliothéconomie scolaire aux niveaux national et international.

La **quatrième partie** présente les références récoltées au cours du projet "Bibliothèques scolaires à travers le monde" dont l'objectif était de recenser les normes et lignes directrices, les politiques, les lois et décrets, les rapports sur la situation des bibliothèques scolaires et tous autres documents de portée générale parus depuis 1980.

La **cinquième partie** signale des ressources récentes en matière de formation à l'usage de l'information et de l'utilisation des technologies de l'information en éducation en relation avec le travail des bibliothécaires et des enseignants-documentalistes en milieu scolaire.

Toutes ces ressources constituent le présent outil que nous sommes heureux de mettre à la disposition de la communauté, au moment où la Section fête ses vingt ans d'existence et son nouveau nom!

Paulette Bernhard, Présidente, Section des bibliothèques et centres documentaires scolaires

---

The book you have in your hands is the result of the work of a group of persons convinced of the importance of resource-based learning and teaching and, consequently, of school libraries and resource centers and those responsible for them. It highlights the activity of the IFLA Section of School Libraries since its very beginning, identifies professional groups as well as listservs involved in school librarianship worldwide, presents the results of several projects conducted by the Section since 1993, and points to resources in two emerging areas.

Part One highlights the activities of the Section, including publications and papers given at Open Sessions.

Part Two identifies associations in school librarianship or sections of broader associations interested in this field around the world, as well as the principal listservs for school librarians and teacher-librarians.

Part Three , as a result of the Project "List of Periodicals in School Librarianship", presents the compilation of national and international periodicals and newsletters in the field of school librarianship.

Part Four presents the references collected during the Project "School Libraries in the World" which aimed at identifying standards and guidelines, policies, laws and decrees, reports of the state of school libraries, and other documents of general scope published since 1980.

Part Five points to resources in the areas of information literacy instruction and use of technologies in education in connection with the work of school librarians and teacher-librarians.

Together, all these resources form a tool that we are pleased to make available to the community, as the Section celebrates its 20th anniversary and new name!

Paulette Bernhard, Chair of the Section of School Libraries and Resource Centers

Première partie / Part One

La Section des bibliothèques scolaires

The Section of School Libraries

~~~

INTERNATIONAL FEDERATION OF LIBRARY ASSOCIATIONS AND INSTITUTIONS. (IFLA) SCHOOL LIBRARY SECTION. HISTORICAL OVERVIEW.
By Anne M. Galler.   May, 1997

The purpose of this paper is to celebrate the 20th anniversary of the School Libraries Section of IFLA, by describing its origin, its achievements its impact on the profession and its current projects and future plans. The author would like to thank the following: Dr. Paulette Bernhard for encouraging her to undertake and eventually complete this project, the IFLA personnel at Headquarters who helped track down some of the missing documents, Dr. Laverne Carroll for her help as well as all the past Chairs of the Section who were kind enough to contribute to this paper.

THE BEGINNINGS. 1973-1980.

Sub-Section of School Libraries, 1973.

It took three years, from the first brainstorming session of an interested group of practising school librarians, educators and other professionals in the field to establish the Section for School Librarians of IFLA. It was important to create this Section within IFLA, because of the international nature of this organization, its consultative status with many non-governmental organizations, and having members (at the time) in over one hundred countries.

Thus, at the General Council Meeting of IFLA, held in Grenoble, in 1973, the Section of Public Libraries recommended that approval be given to the formation of a Sub-Section of the Public Libraries Section to provide for the interests   and needs of school libraries. This was deemed a necessary first steps towards full status as a section at a later date. The General Council of IFLA approved this resolution i.e. to establish a Sub-Section on School Libraries at its Plenary Session in Grenoble, France, on September 1, 1973.

This founding resolution of the Section was introduced by Colin Ray, England, Chairman of the Sub-section on Library Work with Children at a meeting held August 30. A paper, **Unity of the Profession** was given by Dr. Frances Laverne Carroll, USA. Discussion of the paper and the resolution followed. Dr. Carroll was nominated for the Chairmanship of the new Sub-Section before the meeting adjourned. The purpose of the Sub-Section, as stated in the resolution, will be "to provide for the interests and needs of school libraries. The new Sub-Section will provide a structure through which the interest in school librarianship of associations affiliated with IFLA can be channeled. A Secretary, and Advisory Committee of not more than twelve people will be selected, and

6

the first meeting of this group will be during the next IFLA meeting in Washington, DC, November 16-23, 1974. The Advisory Group will explore thoroughly the role of the new Sub-Section at that time. Comments and assistance may be offered to Dr. Carroll."[1]

1974-1976.

The Planning Group agreed to the conditional title of Planning Group for the School Libraries Section pending revision of the Statutes of IFLA in the following year. Two meetings were actually scheduled by the Planning Group for the Washington Conference (1974) as well as tours to school libraries.[2] Thus, IFLA acknowledged, for the first time, the existence of school libraries as an entity. In addition, a booth in the exhibit area made visual materials concerning school libraries available for consultation. Information about tours of school libraries and visits with school librarians was coordinated at this booth.[3] A Mobile Children's Library was also on hand in the parking lot of the Washington Hilton, as a demonstration unit, from noon, November 18 to noon November 20, 1974.

The **Planning Group** and approximately 75 observers met in the Jefferson East Room of the Washington Place Hotel at 9:00 AM on November 19, 1974. Present were: Linda Beeler, Tatjana Blazekovic, Dr. Frances Laverne Carroll, Noelene Hall, Barbara Hann, Sigrun Klara Hannesdottir, Dr.Jean Lowrie, Rosalind McLaughlin, Colin Ray and Pieter J.Van Swigchem. Ms.Barbara Hann was appointed Secretary of the Planning Group. Dr. Carroll chaired the meeting. The second meeting of the School Library **Planning Group** took place on November 20, 1974 in the Farragut Room of the Washington Hilton Hotel, Washington, D.C. The meeting was attended by Margreet Wijnstroom, the General Secretary of IFLA, to explain IFLA's policy in regard to the School Library Planning Group and its relations to the International Association for School Librarianship (IASL) Several members of the Planning Group were present, i.e. Tatjana Blazekovic, Laverne Carroll, Noelene Hall, Barbara Hann, Sigrun Klara Hannesdottir, Jean Lowrie and Rosalind McLaughlin. It was also announced that IASL become a member-association of IFLA. Discussion also took place about differentiating the School Libraries Section from both the Children's Section and college libraries. It was decided that keeping the Section within Division 3, the Division Serving the

---

[1]IFLA NEWS No. 46, November 1973, p.14

[2] IFLA NEWS No. 47, February 1974, p.7

[3] idem, p. 9

General Public, was the right one, and that care should be taken to define the Section adequately, precisely in order to note the differences from both Children and undergraduate college libraries.

The Planning Group met again in Oslo in 1975. As all the other sections, the Planning Group participated in the open meetings where the revision of the IFLA statues were discussed and studied and subsequently approved in Oslo (1976).

At the Professional Board meeting held during the Lausanne Conference (1976) it was

"stressed that School Libraries wanted to be a completely independent section
under the new statues (of IFLA). This was being done with he full knowledge and
approval of both The International Association for School Librarianship (IASL) and
the Planning Group on School Libraries." [4]

By unanimous vote the Professional Board of IFLA decided to recommend to the Executive Board of IFLA the addition of School Libraries as a Section of IFLA, designating Dr. Carroll to continue as Chairperson. The structure of IFLA and the role of a Section within it is described in Appendix "D" of this paper. During this conference, the Planning Group had an activity listed in the official program, but there was no business meeting scheduled as the Section had not yet been officially endorsed by the various levels of the IFLA hierarchy, such as the Professional Board and the Executive Board. The session, with several speakers was very well attended.

1977-1979.

1977 is a most important date, as it marks the the official beginning of the Section, hence the 20th anniversary celebrations during the IFLA General Conference in Copenhagen, Denmark. It is important to note that "The history of the Section for School Libraries" was written for this occasion by Dr Frances Laverne Carroll, and published by IFLA. At the same time it commemorated the 5th anniversary of the World Congress of Librarians held in Bruxelles September 3-10, 1977. Much of the early history of the section is told in great

---

[4] IFLA. Professional Board Minutes. August 28, 1976, pp 4-5

detail in this publication, and will of course not be repeated in this current overview.

The Section on School Libraries was thus officially established by IFLA as a Section in 1977.

The meeting of IFLA on its 50th Anniversary and to honour the World Congress of Librarians (September 3-10, 1977) held in Bruxelles, Belgium, was the appropriate time for the official recognition of the new School Libraries Section of IFLA. Dr. Carroll organized and chaired the Section's first meeting. At this time a new chairperson, Virginia Berkeley, of Bedford, U.K. was also introduced.[5]

Officers of the first Standing Committee, elected for the 1977-1981 period were: Ms.L. Beeleer, Dolton, USA, Secretary and Ms.V.A. Berkeley, Bedford, UK, Chairperson. Members elected were: Ms.B. Dankert, Flensburg, (Germany), K.E.Vance, Ann Arbor, USA, Ms.N.Hall, Australia and Ms.S.K.Hannesdottir, Iceland.

As all other sections, the School Libraries section had the opportunity , according to the IFLA Statutes (23.8.1976) to indicate how many members ift would like to have for the first four hear period, namely no less than five and no more than twenty.

Very early in its existence, the Planning Group already prepared activities of interest to school librarians..

In August 1976, Dr. Carroll put a proposal forward to the Professional Board of IFLA, on behalf of the Planning Group on School Libraries, for a seminar on the education and training of school librarians. According to the IFLA Structure, all activities had and have to be whetted by the Professional Board, which also allocates funding to the various sections it oversees. This seminar eventually took place in December 3-8 1978, in San Juan, Costa Rica, under the leadership of Sigrun Klara Hannesdottir, and was a resounding success. Twenty-one papers (presented in Spanish and subsequently translated into English) were presented at this conference, the theme of which was "The Education of School Librarians in Central America and Panama."

A working group was also formed at that time, to study the "Development of Instructional Materials to assist School Libraries to bring the concept of

---

[5] Carroll, Laverne. History of the School Libraries Section.

information handling and information transfer, to children." Ann Irving of Loughborough University, Loughborough, U.K., was entrusted with the chairing of this Working Group. The Professional Board adopted the proposal, provided it would be submitted in proper form to the Secretary General of UNESCO in time for the General Conference of IFLA to be held in Nairobi. (October /November 1976). The motion was carried with 21 for it and 2 abstentions.

The early period of the Section culminated in the publication co-authored by Dr. Frances Laverne Carroll, and Patricia Beilke, entitled Guidelines for the Planning and Organization of School Media Centers. (1985). The second edition of this publication was edited by Dr. Frances Laverne Carroll, and issued under the following title, in 1990: Guidelines for School Libraries. Also by IFLA.

THE NEXT DECADE, 1980-1990.

Many of the projects proposed during these years have come fruition.
The decade started with the Pre-Session Seminar, held in Leipzig, in 1981, together with the Children's Libraries Section, entitled Library Work with Children and Young People. The seminar was attended by 36 librarians from Africa, Latin America and Asia. The proceedings were edited by Geneviève Patte and Sigrun Klara Hannesdottir and published by IFLA in 1981, entitled Library Work and Young Adults in Developing Countries.

During the 1982 another project was forthcoming to the IFLA Professional Board for funding, entitled "Applications of New Technology to the Educational Function of School Libraries." The idea for this proposal arose from the theme adopted for the Munich (1983) IFLA Conference, i.e. The Impact of Modern Technology on the School Library Information Centre.

The highlight of these years was the full - day seminar held in Nairobi in 1984, during the Annual General Conference of IFLA. This also resulted in an IFLA publication, entitled The School Librarian in an Information Society : Proceedings of the Seminar held by the School Libraries Section during the IFLA General Conference, Nairobi, 1984, edited by Ann Irving.

A Working Group was formed during the Tokyo Conference (1986) to study the Impact of the School Librarians on Academic Achievement. Members were from Canada, Israel, Germany, Japan and New Zealand. Eventually, under the terms of an IFLA Research Grant, a questionnaire was tested in various countries in Asia. The results of this research were presented at the Paris

General Conference of IFLA, by Setsuko Koga and Takashi Harada, entitled "Academic Achievement and the School Library: An international Study".

In 1986 Anne Galler published her handbook entitled Managing School Libraries, also with the help of IFLA funding. This book was co-authored with Joan M. Coulter, and has been translated into French and Spanish. All three volumes were published by IFLA, as part of their Professional Reports series.

The Guidelines for the Education and Training of School Librarians, by Sigrun Klara Hannesdottir first appeared 1986 under the aegis of IFLA. An uptaded edition of this publication also by Hannesdottir, was published by IFLA in 1995, entitled School Librarians, Guidelines for Competency Requirements. Noelene Hall's Teachers, Information and School Libraries, was also published in 1986, by IFLA.

Details of all publications mentioned in this overview can be found in List of Publications of the Section, with all pertinent details.

I would also like to note the fact that in 1988, the first Margareet Wijnstroom Scholarship was awarded to a member of the School Libraries Section, Mr. Otinkorang from Ghana. This enabled Mr. Orinkorang to attend the 1988 IFLA General Conference.The Section was very pleased that one of its members was honoured in this fashion.

CURRENT ACTIVITIES AND PROJECTS, 1990-1997.

The highlight of the current decade of the Section was the 1993 Pre-Conference Seminar held August 15-20 in Caldes de Montbui, Spain. The Seminar, sponsored by UNESCO was a great success, with the attendance of 22 participants from developing countries, as well as a number of observants. Resolutions coming from this seminar were presented to IFLA, and are to be found in APPENDIX "C".

Projects ongoing since 1994 are as follows:

School Libraries in the World - a two year project, approved by IFLA. This project was a direct consequence of the 1993 Pre-Conference in Caldes. Its purpose is to identify and describe standards, guidelines and policies regarding school libraries throughout the world.

List of Periodicals in School Librarianship. This list as the current overview are part of the resource book for school libraries and resource centres as planned.

The following publications, sponsored by the Section appeared during this period:

Guidelines for Conducting National Surveys on School Libraries and Their Needs, by Sigrun Klara Hannesdottir, L.A. Clyde and J. Klobas. The aim of the project was to study current methods of conducting nation-wide surveys of school libraries around the world. The work was conducted under an IFLA contract and published by Unesco in 1994.

School Librarians : Guidelines for Competency Requirements, by Sigrun Klara Hannesdottir. 2nd rev. ed. (formerly published in 1986 as Guidelines for the Education and Training of School Librarians, by IFLA.

Cultural heritage through literature. An annotated bibliography of books from twenty-nine countries. Edited by Lucille C. Thomas. 1993. This publication followed on the footsteps of a Section Project entitled "Promoting Cultural Heritage through Books" within th framework of the Decade of Culture was first proposed during the 1989/90 year. The aim of this activity was to promote better understanding among cultural groups by collecting information about books reflecting the cultural heritage of many countries.

Library Lessons. Suggestions from around the world. Compiled by Blanche Wools. 1993. This publication is also a result of a project entitled "Lessons in the School Library", which was aimed at the collection of library lessons designed by school librarians that contribute to literacy, by motivating reading.

OPEN FORUMS: SPONSORED BY THE DIVISION OF LIBRARIES SERVING THE GENERAL PUBLIC. (DIVISION 3).

The School Libraries Section is one of ten Sections and Round Tables, belonging to this Division. Each Section has a Chair and a Secretary, and together these twenty Officers of IFLA form the Coordinating Board of the Division.

As part of their duty, Chairpersons of the Section have to present, from time to time, the work of the Section at the Open Forum held during the Annual General Conference of IFLA. For example, Anne M. Galler presented a paper during the 1986 Tokyo Conference a paper on the Section, entitled Past, Present and Future of the School Libraries Section. In 1994, Dr. Paulette Bernhard presented to the Open Forum a paper entitled The Section of School Libraries : Goals, Objectives and Actions.

Another important part of the Chairperson and Secretary's work is to attend mid-term meetings of the above-mentioned Coordinating Board of the Division. These meetings are held in March or April, and much work is accomplished at these usually intense two or three day meetings, as to planning, budgeting, formulating projects and strategies.

ACTIVITIES.

Many of the preoccupations and projects of a Section are revealed through its Minutes and Agendas, its Annual Reports as well as through its publications. Very early on, the School Libraries Section realized the importance of communication with its constituency, the school library community, and initiated its Bulletin in December 1977. It was hoped that the Bulletin could be published twice a year. While this was possible in most years in the early days, due to budgetary restrictions, it was not. Its purpose is to convey to members of the Section what happens at any given time in the Section, and to serve as a forum for the exchange of news and information about school libraries around the world.. It also prints the program for the annual conference usually in the spring issue and then reports on the conference in the fall Bulletin.

Over the years the Bulletin evolved from a one-page xeroxed publication into a handsome, computer-produced Newsletter. It is distributed to all members of the Section, but also included interested parties who have participated in IFLA Conferences all over the world. Incidentally, the activities of the Section are available on IFLA-Net, as follows:

http://www.nlc-bnc.ca/ifla/VII/s11ssl.htm

The Section also publishes an attractive Brochure, which is translated into some of the official IFLA languages, notably French and Spanish. Most recently the brochure has been translated into Italian and Chinese - the latter in connection with the conference being held in China (1996).The brochure describes the work of the Section, its position within the IFLA Structure, mentions future conference sites, describes the most recent publications of the section, and of course mentions its current officers. IFLA encourages each Section to put out its own brochure.

Conference papers and other publications.

During its twenty years existence the Section has always presented papers many of which resulted in publications either in the IFLA journal, or in other important library publications. Some of these are highlighted in this paper, but an exhaustive list of all monographs, professional publications, significant to the school library community are available in the List of Publications attached to this document.

MISSION OF THE SCHOOL LIBRARIES SECTION

IFLA over the years has instituted a 5 year plan, called MEDIUM TERM PROGRAMMES OF IFLA. These include a mission statement from each section as well as the plan of action for the ensuing period. At present a two-year time-table is attached to the medium term program, to make sure that the sections adhere to their programs. Another important part of the 5 year plan is the evaluation of the work accomplished, to take place after each two-year period.

14

Medium Term Programme, 1975-1980.	Medium Term Programme, 1981-1985.	Medium Term Programme, 1986-1991.	Merium Term Programme, 1992-1997.
As early as 1975, when the Section was still a sub-section of the Public Libraries, the Planning group submitted a mission statement concerning school libraries, to be included in the medium Term Programme of IFLA "Although in some countries school librarians have long been recognized as a special branch of the library profession, in many others the emergence of the school librarian as distinct from a teacher with the responsibility for a library, is a recent occurrence or has not yet taken place. For this reason school librarianship had held no place until quite recently in IFLA's organization."	This is the first time that the Section submitted an official mission statement to IFLA, as follows: "Libraries in primary and secondary schools are essential to the maintenance of educational and cultural life. School libraries provide materials which support the curriculum and assist in the achievement of the educational goals of teacher and pupils. This is a widely accepted role, but increasingly school libraries are recognised as contributing to a nation's library resources and playing a vital role in educating library users of the future. In developing countries the majority of the literate population may be found in schools, although in some countries many children do not have the opportunity to progress beyond the primary stage. It is therefore particularly important that libraries in primary schools are well provided for. Providing adequate library services in schools may be the first step in providing nation-wide library services."	The Section of School Libraries comes under Division 3, Libraries Serving the General Public. It is one of six Sections and four Round Tables. Its aims and objectives are: 1. Promotion of school library services to ensure that they meet the needs of all user groups. 2. Delienation of the role of school libraries at the international level. 3. Increasing the exchange of information between school libraries and other types of libraries. 4. Fostering research in the field of school librarianship and assisting school librarians in their professional developments 5. Enhancing the image of the school librarian.	The Section of School Libraries comes under Division 3, Libraries Serving the General Public. Its aims and objectives are described as follows: Promotion of school library services in all parts of the world to ensure that they meet the needs of all user groups. Delineation of the role of school libraries. Promotion of the role of school libraries. Promotion of research in the field of school librarianship. Encouragement of initial training and continuing education of school librarians. Enhancement of the image of the school librarian. Goals for the same 5 years are as follows: Show how academic achievement is influenced by an effective school library programme. Promote the role of school libraries in the cultural dimension of society. Help school librarians improve their skills.

Achievements of the medium term programmes.

Each 5-year term is summed up at the end by a review. According to Mr.PJ van Swigchem author for this period 1981-1985 there were several developments regarding School Libraries,

The Liverpool meeting (1991) saw the beginning of the pre-conference seminars and workshops, mainly aimed at developing countries, and sponsored by UNESCO, or other non-governmental as well as governmental organizations. Seminar number 10 is of particular interest, as its theme was "Library work with children and young adults."

In this review Mr. van Swigchem also refers to other projects in developing countries that concerned schools, such as "An experiment with home libraries in Zimbabwe" and "School libraries for blind children in Sierra Leone" and the "Development of reading in Senegal." as well as the the very important "Seminar on the Education of School Librarians in Central America and Panama" held in San Jose, Costa Rica, in 1978, organized by Sigrun Klara Hannesdottir under the aegis of IFLA.

Mr. van Swigchem further states that in the Section of School Libraries, particular attention has been given to the planning and development of school library media centres for which guidelines had been published by UNESCO in 1979.

In a curious fashion it was during this period that the Audio-Visual Round Table was formed, under the Division of Libraries Serving the General Public, which also houses the Section for School libraries. However, for reasons of its own IFLA decided to place the Round Table for Audio-Visual services within the Division of Management and Technology. The RT is still there, although it is felt that it has definitely more affinity with the Division of Libraries Serving the General Public, where Children's and Schools are located.

This review by van Swigchem also refers to the Seminar on the Education of School Librarians in Central America and Panama, held in San Jose, Costa Rica, in 1978.

ANNUAL MEETINGS.

Many of the SC projects are discussed during the annual meetings. Since elections take place every two years, during the Annual Conference, there is sometimes a lack of continuity as new officers with new ideas and goals take over. Both the Secretary and Chair are elected for two years, but may be re-elected for another two. As work within IFLA tends to be slow, precisely because it is such a huge international organisation, and because of the infrequency of meetings, even when officers stay in their positions for four years, it is not always possible to accomplish what they set out to do within the period they act as officers.

It is also possible to have brief executive meetings during the deliberations of the Coordinating Board, when they take place in March and April, as well as during the annual conference, especially if both the Chair of a Section and the Secretary are able to attend these mid-year CB meetings. It is desirable, but not always possible to try and arrange for a meeting of some additional Section Standing Committee members, if they live within a reasonable distance from the location of such a meeting. As most of the burden of the work is carried on by the Chair and the Secretary, who is in addition groomed to take over eventually as Chair, again to allow continuity, Such meetings have successfully taken place in the past and have been helpful.

The following members have been Chairs of the Section since the Section was officially inaugurated.

Chairs of the Section	Secretaries of the Section
1973	Barbara Hann (Canada)
1973-75 Frances Laverne Carroll (U.S.)	Linda Beeler (U.S.)
1975-77 Frances Laverne Carroll	Barbara Eddy (U.S.)
1977-79 Virginia Berkeley (U.K.)	Linda Beeler (U.S.)
1979-81 Virginia Berkeley (U.K.)	Birgit Dankert (Germany)
1981-83 Ann Irving (U.K.)	Noelene Hall (Australia)
1983-85 Ann Irving (U.K.)	Birgit Danker (Germany)
1985-87 Anne M. Galler (Canada)	Lucille Thomas (U.S.)
1987-89 Anne M. Galler (Canada)	Lucille Thomas (U.S.)
1989-91 Lucille Thomas (U.S.A.)	Astrid Lauster (Germany)
1991-93 Lucille Thomas (U.S.A.)	Astrid Lauster (Germany)
1993-95 Paulette Bernhard (Canada)	Torny Kjerkstad (Norway)
1995-97 Paulette Bernhard (Canada)	Torny Kjerkstad (Norway)

I feel that while much has been achieved in the relatively brief, twenty-year history of the Section of School Libraries, thanks to the devotion and single-mindedness of its members, Chairs and Secretaries, much still has to be achieved. While school libraries are developing in one part of the world, they are also threatened in others.

Thus we will have to be forever vigilant, in order to maintain, strengthen and improve the position of school libraries and school librarians.

I would like to end this brief history with a quote of one of its founders, Dr. Frances Laverne Carroll:

"The inclusion of school librarianship into the broad interpretation of the profession of librarianship is a timely activity for IFLA. School libraries are in a growth stage around the world and will influence other libraries and education. The unity of school librarianship as well as of librarianship as a whole is threatened by the new media, a time lag in library education and the organization of documentalists. Unity is defined.to mean cooperation, not conformity."[7]

---

[7] Carroll, Frances Laverne. The Unity of the Profession. IFLA Paper. 1973. p.1

ENDNOTES

Bernhard, Paulette. "The Section of School Libraries: Goals, Objectives and Actions." Presentation at the OPEN FORUM OF DIVISION 3. IFLA 1994, Havana, Cuba, 5p.

Bernhard, Paulette. "The Status of School Library Media Services Through IFLA: Report to IASL Assembly of Associations. IASL 25th Conference. July 1996. 4p.

Carroll, Frances Laverne. "The raison d'être of IFLA' School Library Section." The Journal of Library History. v. 12, no.4, Fall 1977, pp.364-376.

Carroll, Frances Laverne. The Unity of the Profession. 39th General Council of IFLA Grenoble, 30 August 1973. 15p.

Carroll, Frances Laverne. "Planning Group on School Libraries." International Library Review. (1976) 8. p.451-452.

Galler, Anne M. "Past, Present and Future of the School Library Section of IFLA. IFLA General Conference. Tokyo, Japan, 1986. 8p.

Galler, Anne M. "Past, Present and Future of School Librarianship and the School library Section of IFLA. Tokyo, Japan, 1986. 10p.

Hannesdottir, Sigrun Klara. "Education of School Librarians: Some Alternatives." IFLA JOURNAL, v.6 (1980) 1.

Hope, E.A. Clement. Work Plans of IFLA Professional Groups - 1992-1997. The Hague, IFLA, 1992.

Knuth, Rebecca. "School Librarianship and Macro-Level Policy Issues: International Perspectives." IFLA Journal, v.21 (4) (1995). 290-298.

IFLA School Libraries Section. Annual Reports. !977-1996.

IFLA School Libraries Section. Newsletters. 1977-1996.

Meacham, M. "Development of School Libraries Around the World." International Library Review. v.8 (1976) 453-459.

van Swigchem, P.J. IFLA and the Library World. A Review of the Work of IFLA, 1981-1985. The Hague, IFLA, 1985.

1.2
LISTE DES PUBLICATIONS DE LA SECTION DES BIBLIOTHÈQUES SCOLAIRES

LIST OF PUBLICATIONS OF THE SECTION OF SCHOOL LIBRARIES

Par / By :   Paulette Bernhard   et / and   Anne Galler

INTRODUCTION

La liste ci-dessous recense les publications de la Section. Elle ne mentionne pas les documents internes tels que le bulletin et les rapports annuels. Nous vous remercions d'avance de bien vouloir nous faire part des oublis et erreurs que vous seriez amenés à constater.

You will find below the references to the publications of the Section. Internal documents such as the Newsletter and annual reports are not listed. We thank you in advance for notifying us of any error or omission that you notice.

Actes de congrès et séminaires / Conference and Seminar Proceedings

Hannesdottir, Sigrun Klara (ed. and transl.) *Education of school librarians : some alternatives papers presented at the Seminar for the Education of School Librarians for Central America and Panama at San Jose, Costa Rica, Dec. 3-8, 1978.* München : K.G. Saur, 1982. 120 p. (Fédération internationale des associations de bibliothécaires et des bibliothèques. IFLA publications; 22)

Irving, Ann (Ed.) *The School librarian in an information society : proceedings of the seminar held by the School Libraries Section during the IFLA General Conference, Nairobi, 1984.* Loughborough: Section on School Libraries, International Federation of Library Associations and Institutions, 1985. vii, 63 p. (Fédération internationale des associations de bibliothécaires et des bibliothèques. Section des bibliothèques scolaires)

Patte, Geneviève; Hannesdottir, Sigrun Klara (Eds.) *Library work for children and young adults in the developing countries: proceedings of the IFLA/ UNESCO pre-session seminar in Leipzig, GDR, 10-15 August, 1981 = Les enfants, les jeunes et les bibliothèques dans les pays en développement : actes du séminaire IFLA/UNESCO de Leipzig, RDA, 10-15 aout, 1981.* München : K.G. Saur, 1984. 283 p. (Fédération internationale des associations de bibliothécaires et des bibliothèques. IFLA publications; 28) ISBN 3598203896

Proceedings of the IFLA Pre-session seminar on School Librarianship: Issues for Developing Countries, August15-20, 1993, Caldes de Montbui, Spain. To be issued in 1997. (Fédération internationale des associations de bibliothécaires et des bibliothèques. IFLA publications)

Dans la collection / From the series : *IFLA Professional Reports*

Carroll, Frances Laverne. *Guidelines for school libraries.* The Hague: IFLA, 1990. 40 p. (IFLA professional reports; 20) ISBN 90-70916-24-X
Note: translated into Italian (1995) and Arabic (1996)

Galler, Anne M.; Coulter, Joan. *La administracionde las bibliotecas escolares.* The Hague: IFLA, 1991. (IFLA professional reports; 29) ISBN 90-7096-32-0

Galler, Anne M.; Coulter, Joan. *La bibliohèque scolaire: administration, organisation et services.* The Hague: IFLA, 1990. (IFLA professional reports; 23) ISBN 90-70916-27-4

Galler, Anne M.; Coulter, Joan. *Managing school libraries.* The Hague: IFLA, 1989. 68 p. (IFLA professional reports; 17) ISBN 90-70916-21-5

Hannesdottir, Sigrun Klara (Ed. and comp.) *Guidelines for the education and training of school librarians.* The Hague: IFLA, 1986. 47 p. (IFLA professional reports; 9) ISBN 90-70916-12-6

Hannesdottir, Sigrun Klara. *School librarians : guidelines for competency requirements.* The Hague: IFLA, 1995. 50 p. (IFLA professional reports; 41) ISBN 90-70916-57-6.
(Note: Mise à jour du document no 9 / Updates document no 9 issued in1986 under the title: *Guidelines for the education and training of school librarians*)

Documents élaborés conjointement avec le Programme Général d'Information de l'UNESCO / Documents prepared in collaboration with the UNESCO General Information Programme

Carroll, Frances Laverne; Beilke, Patricia. *Guidelines for the planning and organization of school media centers.* Rev. ed. Paris: UNESCO, 1979. 55 p. (PGI-79/WS/17)

Carroll, Frances Laverne; Beilke, Patricia F. *Directives pour la conception et l'organisation de médiathèques scolaires.* Ed. rev. Paris : Unesco, 1979. 55 p. (PGI-79/WS/17) (Organisation des nations Unies pour l'éducation, la science et la culture. Programme général d'information)

Hall, Noelene. *Teachers, information and school libraries.* Prepared for the IFLA Section on School Libraries Working Group. Paris : General Information Programme and UNISIST, United Nations Educational, Scientific and Cultural Organization, 1986. 110 p. (PGI-86/WS/17) (Fédération internationale des associations de bibliothécaires et des bibliothèques. Section des bibliothèques scolaires. Groupe de travail)

Hall, Noelene. *Les enseignants, l'information et les bibliothèques scolaires.* Étude rédigée pour le Groupe de travail de la Section des bibliothèques scolaires de l'IFLA. Paris : UNESCO Programme général d'information : Unisist, 1986. viii-89 p. (Fédération internationale des associations de bibliothécaires et des bibliothèques. Section des bibliothèques scolaires. Groupe de travail)

Hannesdottir, Sigrun Klara (Ed.). *Guidelines for conducting national surveys of school libraries and their needs.* Paris: UNESCO, 1994. 115 p. (CII-94/WS/7)

Irving, Anne. *Instructional materials for developing information concept and information handling skills in school children: an international study.* Paris: UNESCO, 1981. ii-64 p. (PGI-81/WS/32).

Irving, Anne. *Promoting voluntary reading to children and young people: guidelines for teacher training courses.* Paris: UNESCO, 1980. ISBN 92-3-101844-2

Autres documents / Other documents

Library lessons. Suggestions from around the world developed by the School Library Section, International Federation of Library Associations and Institutions. The Hague: International Federation of Library Associations, Section of School Libraries, 1993. 19 p.

Thomas, Lucille C. (Ed.) *Cultural heritage through literature. Annotated bibliography of books from twenty-nine countries.* The Hague: International Federation of Library Associations, Section of School Libraries, 1993. iii-22 p.

1.3

LISTE DES CONFÉRENCES - par année

LIST OF PAPERS - per year

Par / By : Anne Galler, Paulette Bernhard

Avec la collaboration de :   With the collaboration of :
Mary Collis, Margaret Tye, Guylaine Vinet, Glenys Willars, Blanche Woolls

INTRODUCTION

Nous signalons dans les pages qui suivent les quelque 110 communications faites durant les rencontres publiques et les ateliers lors des congrès de l'IFLA, ainsi que lors des pré-séminaires organisés par la Section des bibliothèques scolaires. Étant donné que nous avons établi cette liste en recoupant les nombreuses mais souvent incomplètes informations dont nous disposions, nous vous remercions d'avance de bien vouloir nous faire part des erreurs ou oublis qui n'auront pas manqué de se produire.

You will find in the following list the references to about 110 papers given at open sessions and workshops during the IFLA conferences, as well as during the pre-session seminars organized by the Section of School Libraries. Considering that this list has been established by comparing the numerous but often incomplete lists that were available, we thank you in advance for notifying us of all errors and omissions that you notice.

1973 - Grenoble (39th) - Planning Group for School Library Work

Carroll, Frances Laverne. The unity of the profession. 1973.

Cholov, Peter. Essence and specificity of school libraries. 1973.

1976 - Lausanne (42nd) - Planning Group on School Libraries

Baker, P. School and public library programs and information dissemination. 1976. (8/A/BSC/1A)

Blazekovic, R. The professional education of school libraries. 1976.

Scherrer, Lucia. The conversion of secondary school libraries into multimedia centres: an experience in the Canton of Geneva. 1976. (10/A/BSC/IC)

Vance, K.; Baker, P.; Blazekovic, R.; Scherrer, L. Information dissemination through school and public libraries. 1976.

1977 - Brussels (43rd) - Section of School Libraries
Theme: User Education in School Libraries

Droog, Jan. The education of the information user. 1977. (40/E,R/SCH/1)

Ogunsheye, F. Adetowun. An experiment in library and information service to primary schools: the case of Abadina-Nigeria. 1977. (64/E/SCH/2)

Sikorsky, N.M. Libraries and education. 1977.

1978 - Strbské Pleso (44th) - Theme: School Libraries and their contribution to UAP

de Horowitz, Rosario Gassol. The school library and NATIS in developing countries: the need for integration. 1978. (23/SCHO/1E)

Dyer, E.R. Including school libraries in national bibliographic systems. 1978.

Gyebi, Alfred.K. School libraries as part of a national library network: the relevance of experience in Ghana to other developing countries. 1978. (3/SCHO/4E)

Irving, Ann. Educating library users in schools. 1978. (31/SCHO/3E)

1979 - Copenhagen (45th)

Bredsdorff, Aase. Practical aspects of school library legislation. 1979. (59/SCHO/2 E)

Dankert, Birgit. Political aspects of school library legislation. 1979.

Johansen, Anna. AV media in library legislation. 1979. (39/SCHO/1)

1980 - Manila (46th)

Aggaoili, Candida C. Developing and exchanging learning materials for greater international understanding. 1980. (59/SCHO/1E)

Beilke, B.F. School libraries and priorities for development: selected comments. 1980.

Temu, Deveni. Extending school library and community information services to a scatered population: Papua New Guinea. 1980. (60/SCHO/2E)

Paper presented under the aegis of the Section of Children'sLibraries:

Ganitskaya, I.I. Children's and school libraries in the unified system of library service of children and juveniles. 1980.

1981 - Leipzig (47th)

Irving, Ann. Information concepts and skills for school children: an international study on instructional materials and their development. 1981. (65/CHIL/3 E and 65/SCHO/1)

Jones, Arthur. Standards, objectives and guidelines for school libraries. 1981. (78/SCHO/2 E)

Professional meeting on the Contribution of School Librarianship to Professional Library Activities:

El-Hush, A.M. Development of libraries and information centers: present and future in the Jarmahiriya. 1981.

Joint meeting with Section of Children's Libraries:

Irving, Ann. The contribution of user education in school libraries in preparing children for all library skills. 1981.

Koldenius, M. Children's library users - are they adults? 1981.

1982 - Montréal (48th)

Joint meeting with the Round Table of National Centres for Library Services:

Adcock, Donald. C. School libraries and networking in North America: principles and problems of participation. 1982. (98/SCHO/ROTNAC/1-E)
(Les bibliothèques d'école et le réseau des bibliothèques en Amérique du Nord: principes et problèmes de participation)

Erikstad, C. The contribution of national centres to networking in school libraries. 1982.

Reumer, Dick. The centralized automation of national centres to networking in school libraries. 1982. (129/SCHO/ROTNAC/2-E)
(L'automatisation centralisée des Centres Nationaux du réseau des bibliothèques d'écoles)

1983 - Munich (49th)

School Libraries joint program with Children's Libraries and AV Media - Theme: Information technology for school children

Beck, Jean. C. Information technology for schoolchildren. 1983. (SCHO-1-40-AVM-2-E CHIL-1)

Papendieck, Andreas. Schulbibliotheken und Schulmediotheken in der Bundesrepublic Deutschland. 1983. (106-CHIL-5/SCHO-3/AVM-4-G)
(New environment of learning through school library media centers in the Federal Republic of Germany)

Sylla, Fatimata. Senegal and information technology: the pilot research project "Information technology and education with the LOGO language". 1983. (AVM-3/ 102-2-F/CHIL-3)

1984 - Nairobi (50th)

Hannesdottir, Sigrun Klara & others. The school librarian in information society: an outline of competency requirements. 1984.

Helle, M. Using the school library. 1984.

Mwathi, P.G.; Ng'ang'a, D.G. School libraries in Africa: an overview. 1984.

Papers given at a one-day seminar during conference week:

Hannesdottir, Sigrun Klara. The education and training of school librarians: an international study. 1984.

Line, Maurice. UAP and school libraries. 1984.

Matiba, the Honourable Kenneth, M.P. Welcome and Address from the Minister for Culture and Social Services. 1984.

Mwathi, Peter. School libraries in perspective. 1984.

1985 - Chicago (51st)

Hannesdottir, Sigrun Klara. Guidelines for the education and training of school librarians. 1985. (180-SCHO-3-E)

Hall, Noelene. Teachers, information and school libraries. 1985. (180-SCHO-1-E)

Dankert, Birgit. Effective management and use of secondary school libraries. 1985. (180-SCHO-2-E)

1986 - Tokyo (52nd)

Galler, Anne M. How a typical Canadian elementary school library is run in a busy metropolitan area. 1986. (057-SCHO-1-E)

Gawith, Gwen. School libraries: bridges or barriers ? 1986. (055-SCHO-1-E)

Kasahara, Yoshiro. School libraries in Japan. Present status and problems of school libraries in Japan: in order to achieve educational excellence. (Slide presentation) 1986. (204-SCHO-4-E)

Koyama, Ikuko. The guidance of reading and information skills in school libraries: Japan's case, 1986. (106-SCHO-3-E)

Presentation at Division 3:

Galler, Anne M. Past, present and future of the School Library Section of IFLA. 1986. (056-GENPU-2-E+J)

1987 - Brighton (53rd)

Breithaupt, Renate. Zentrale Dienstleistungen fuer Schulbibliotheken in der Bundesrepublik Deutschland am Beispiel des Schulbibliothekarischen Arbeitsstelle der Stadbucherei Frankfurt am Main. 1987. (Centralized school library services in the Federal Republic of Germany as performed at the School Library Services Centre of the Stadbucherei Frankfurt am Main)

de Molinare Naveillan, Teresa; Soto, Yolande. The current situation of school libraries in South America with special reference to Chile. 1987.

Horn, Ann. School libraries of Norway: a vital part of the national library network? 1987.

Mathews, Anne J. Excellence on a budget: school library services with limited resources. 1987.

1988 - Sydney (54th)

Andrews, Gail. The Maori dimension in New Zealand schools. 1988. (10-SCHOOL-2-E)

Cane, Georgina. The Australian Schools Catalogue Information Service (ASCIS): its environment, clients and services. 1988. (60-SCHOOL-3-E)
(Avstralijskaja Informacionnaja Sluzba Dlja skolínyh katalogov - ASCIS)

Thomas, Lucille. Multiculturalism: challenges and opportunities for school librarians. 1988. (6-SCHOOL-1-E)

1989 - Paris (55th)

Bernhard, Paulette. Theoretical foundations of the school library/media centre and their implications for education, 1989.
(De quelques fondements théoriques de la bibliothèque/mÈdiathèque en milieu scolaire et de leurs implications pédagogiques)

Koga, Setsuko. Academic achievement and the school library: an international study. 1989. (031-SCHOOl-3-E+F+S)
(Résultats scolaires et bibliothèques scolaires: une étude internationale; Resulados academicas y bibliotecas escolares: un estudio internacional)

Valin, Anne. Pédagogie de la lecture en zone rurale. 1989. (018-SCHOOL-2-F+E+S)
(Pedagogy of reading in a rural area; Pedagogia de la lectura en zona rural

1990 - Stockholm (56th) - Theme: Literacy and the School Library

Christensen, Jytte. The difference and the likeness between the school library and the public library in Denmark. 1990.

Stenberg, Christina. Literacy and the school library: librarians and teachers together against illiteracy. 1990 . (48-SCHOOL-2-E)

Woolls, Blanche. Literacy and school libraries. 1990. (47-SCHOOL-1-E)

1991 - Moscow (57th) - Theme: Heritage through Literature

Rande, Anne. How literature is used with children to promote cultural heritage and cultural appreciation. 1991. (122-SCHOOL-2E)

Tsesarskaja, G. L. Kulturnoe nasledie: literatura junosestvu. 1991. (068-SCHOOl-1-R+E+S)
(Cultural heritage through literature.) (El legado cultural a traves de la literatura)

1992 - New Delhi (58th) - Theme: Meeting information Needs of Slow, Average and Gifted Learners

Kapoor, Malati. Meeting information needs of slow, average and gifted learners. 1992. (016-SCHOOL-1-E)

Sen, Bandana. Meeting the needs of students at an international school. 1992. (017-SCHOOL-2-E)

1993 - Barcelona (59th) - Theme: Literacy, literature and learning

Celler, Zsuzsanna. Literacy, literature and learning in school libraries in Hungary. 1993. (074-SCHOOL-E)

Hannesdottir, Sigrun. Reading habits of children (in Iceland). 1993.

Pre-Session Seminar on School Librarianship : Issues for Developing Countries

Dike, Virginia W. Issues in school librarianship in the developing countries. 14 p.

Faseh, Mary. Issues in stocking school libraries. 23 p.

Hannesdottir, Sigrun Klara. Survey Research in School Librarianship. Report on Guidelines for Conducting National Surveys on School Libraries and Their Needs. 16 p.

Isaza de Pedraza, Mary Luz. El financiamiento de las bibliotecas escolares en paises en desarrollo. 34 p.

Singh, Diljit. An International Comparative Study of School Libraries. 2 p.

Zachary Pretlow, Delores. Management Issues in School Librarianship. 12 p.

DEVELOPING COUNTRIES:

Argentina. Cordoba, Carlos A. La biblioteca escolar en Argentina informe de situacion. 4 p.

China. Dong, Xiaoying; Zhang, Shuhua. Report of School Libraries in China. 6 p.

Brazil. Fragoso, Graça Maria. Bibliothèque scolaire où êtes-vous? 14 p.

Chile. Faundez Garcia, Paola Violeta. Las bibliotecas escolares en Chile. 21 p.+annexes+Programa mece : orientaciones basicas, objetivos y componentes. 40 + 10 p.

Colombia. Isaza de Pedraza, Mary Luz. Informe sobre las bibliotecas escolares en Colombia.

Cuba. Chomat, Mercedes Alfonso. Las bibliotecas escolares en Cuba: un recurso para la educacion. 5 p.

Ethiopia. Muhudien, Mohammed. Country Report. Ethiopia. 7 p.

Estonia. Raatma, Irma. Views of estonian school libraries. 8 p. + 1 tabl.

Fiji. Prasad, Humesh. Country paper : Fiji school library services in Fiji. 12 p. + 1 carte

Hungary. Celler, Zsuzsanna. School libraries in Hungary. 5 p. + 1 tabl.

India. Powdwal, Sushama. School libraries in India : a country report. 14 p. + 3 annexes

Jamaica. Anderson Beatrice L. School libraries in Jamaica. A short report. 11 p.

Jordan. Faseh, Mary. Country Report. Jordan. 4 p.

Lebanon. Kaidbey, Leila Hassan. School library in Lebanon. 5 p. + 4 p. annexes

Malaisia. Singh, Diljit. Country report : Malaysia. 5 p.

Myanmar/Birmanie. Hla Soe Soe. School libraries of Myanmar. 7 p.

Namibia. Tötemeyer, Andree-Jeanne. School libraries in Namibia. 12 p. + 9 p. annexes

Papua New Guinea. Paraide, Daniel. School libraries in Papua New Guinea. 12 p.

Sénégal. Corréa, Antoinette F. Les programmes de bibliothèques en milieu scolaire. 47 p.

Swaziland. Tawete, Felix K. The state of school libraries in Swaziland. 12 p.

Tunisia. Fettahi, Ali. Les bibliothèques scolaires en Tunisie. 10 p.

Zimbabwe. Stringer, Roger. Report on the compilation and publication of the Directory of Zimbabwe Publishers. 4 p.

DEVELOPPED COUNTRIES:

Australia. Nicholson, Fay. An overview of the current situation in school libraries. 20 p.

Spain. Baro, Mònica; Manà, Teresa. Aproximacion al estado actual de las bibliotecas escolares en Espana. 10p.

United States. Zachary Pretlow, Delores.United States of America School Library Media Programs. 3 p.

1994 - La Havane (60th) - Theme: School Libraries in Cooperation with Other Libraries

Bernhard, Paulette. La coopération entre bibliothèques scolaires et bibliothèques publiques et un mot sur les bibliothèques combinées. 1994.

Chomat, Mercedes Alfonso; Crespo, Idelio Rojas. La biblioteca escolar en Cuba: un recurso para la educacion. 1994.

Kjekstad, Torny. Outline of the Norwegian guidelines for school libraries. 1994.

Urquhart, Felix. The development of the school library system in Cuba. 1994.

Presentation at Division 3:

Bernhard, Paulette. The section of school libraries: goals, objectives, and actions, 1994.

Presentation at Joint Workshop (Public Libraries, Libraries serving multicultural populations and Children's Libraries) - Theme: Library Services for Young Adults

Kjekstad, Torny. Cooperation and educational aspects : library services for young adults: Norwegian cooperation projects between public and school libraries. 1994.

1995 - Istanbul (61st) - Theme: Planning for School Libraries for the Future

Hannesdottir, Sigrun Klara. What do school librarians need to know ?: guidelines for competency requirements. 1995. (073-SCHOOL-2-E)

Hay, Lyn; Henri, James. Leadership for collaboration: making vision work. 1995.

Önal, Inci. The future roles and functions of the school libraries: a project for Turkish school libraries. 1995. (oo9-SCHOOL-1-E)

Vernotte, France. La bibliothèque scolaire, outil de formation à l'information: l'exemple français; les CDI des établissements scolaires. 1995. (080-SCHOOL-3F)

1996 - Beijing (62nd) - Theme: Cooperation and Planning with Teachers

Charrier, Colette. Le CDI, outil pédagogique des enseignants: pour une mise en place d'une formation à l'information en équipe professeur-documentaliste. 1996.
(The Documentation and Information center, a pedagogical tool for teachers: towards implementing information literacy education through cooperation between teachers and school librarians)

Horikawa, Teruyo. The types and levels of the cooperation with teachers in the high school libraries in Japan. 1996.

Xiaobin, Jia; Yunxiang, Du; Aiqin Si; Xiaoyan, Zhang. China's primary and secondary school libraries: their history, status quo and future. 1996.

1997 - To be presented in Copenhagen (63rd) - Theme: School libraries as a basis for lifelong learning

Sørensen, Ivan. School libraries as a basis for lifelong learning. 1997.

Herring, James E. The Information Skills: the PLUS approach - a view from the UK. 1997.

Chapron, Françoise. Les CDI (Centre de Documentation et d'Information) des lycées et collèges en France: quelle contribution à la formation du citoyen ? 1997.
(French Resource Centers (CDIs) in secondary school: what contribution for training citizens?)

Karila, Ulla; Rissanen, Raissa. Flexible Learning Environments (FLE) Project. 1997.

Galler, Anne M.; Giguère, Marlene; Locke, Joanne; Darwent, S. Information literacy: a prototype to be used in school libraries. 1997.

Presentation at Division 3:

Bernhard, Paulette. Les bibliothèques scolaires: des centres d'information et de ressources. 1997.
(School libraries as information and resource centers).

1.3
LISTE DES CONFÉRENCES - index des auteurs
LIST OF PAPERS - Index of Authors

Deuxième partie / Part Two

~~~

Associations et listes de discussion en bibliothéconomie scolaire

~~~

Associations and Listservs in School Librarianship

~~~

Par / by : Paulette Bernhard

avec la collaboration de :   with the collaboration of :
Guylaine Vinet

2.1 Associations
- Index des pays / Index of Countries
- Liste alphabétique / Alphabetical List

2.2 Principales listes de discussion
Principal Listservs

2.1

ASSOCIATIONS - Index par pays / Index of Countries

Par / By Paulette Bernhard

Avec la collaboration de :   With the collaboration of :
Guylaine Vinet

INTERNATIONAL	- Fédération internationale des associations de bibliothécaires et des bibliothèques / International Federation of Library Associations and Institutions (IFLA) - Section des bibliothèques et centres documentaires scolaires / Section of School Libraries and Resource Centers - International Association of School Librarianship (IASL)
AFRIQUE DU SUD / SOUTH AFRICA	- South African School Media Association
AUSTRALIE / AUSTRALIA	- Australian Library and Information Association (ALIA) - School Libraries Section - Australian School Library Association (National) . Australian School Library Association (ACT) . Australian School Library Association (NSW) . School Library Association of Northern Territory . School Library Association of Queensland (SLAQ) . School Library Association of Victoria (SLAV) . South Australia School Library Association (SASLA) . Tasmania. Australian School Library Association (TAS) . Western Australia School Library Association
BOTSWANA	- Botswana Library Association - Group for School Libraries
BRÉSIL / BRAZIL	- Federaçao Brasileira de Associaoes de Bibliotecarios
CANADA	- Association for Media and Technology in Education in Canada (AMTEC) - Association for Teacher-Librarianship in Canada (ATLC) - Canadian School Library Association (CSLA) . Alberta Learning Resources Council . British Columbia Teacher-Librarians' Association (BCTLA) . Manitoba School Library Association (MSLA) . New Brunswick. Library Council of the New Brunswick Teachers Association (dissolution to come in June 1997) . Newfoundland Learning Resources Council . North West Territories (NWTTALRC) . Nova Scotia School Library Association (NSSLA) . Ontario School Library Association (OSLA) . Prince Edward Island Teacher-Librarian's Association (PEITLA) . Québec. Association du personnel des services documentaires scolaires . Québec. Quebec Library Association. School Libraries Section . Saskatchewan School Library Association (SSLA) . Saskatchewan Library Association (Sask. Teachers Federation) . Yukon LTA
CHILI / CHILE	- Association for School and Public Librarians
CROATIE / CROATIA	- Croatian Library Association - Committee for School Libraries
DANEMARK / DENMARK	- Danmarks Skolebiblioteksforening / The Danish School Library Association - The Danish Association of School Librarians
ÉGYPTE / EGYPT	- Egyptian School Library Association
ESPAGNE / SPAIN	- Associacion Educacion y Biblioteca

ÉTATS-UNIS / **UNITED STATES**	- American Library Association - American Association of School Librarians (AASL) - Association for Educational Communications and Technology (AECT) . pour les sections AASL et AECT dans les différents États, voir / for AASL and AECT Sections in individual States, see: *School library media annual* (1994)
ÉTHIOPIE / ETHIOPIA	- Committee for the Development of School-Community Library for Children
FRANCE	- Fédération des Enseignants Documentalistes de l'Éducation nationale (FADBEN) - CEDIS
GHANA	- Ghana Library Association - Ghana School Library Association
HONG KONG	- Hong Kong Teacher-Librarians' Association
HONGRIE / HUNGARY	- Hungarian Teacher Librarian Association
ILES FIJI / FIJI ISLANDS	- Fiji Library Association - School Libraries Interest Group
INDE / INDIA	- Indian Library Association - Central Sectional Committee for School Libraries
INDONÉSIE / INDONESIA	- Majala IPI. School Library Division
ITALIE / ITALY	- Ente Nazionale per la Biblioteche Poplari e Scolastiche
JAMAÏQUE / JAMAICA	- Jamaica Library Association (JLA) - School Libraries Section
JAPON / JAPAN	- Japan School Library Association
MALAISIE / MALAySIA	- Library Association of Malaysia - School Library Committee - Malaysian Educational Technology Association
NIGÉRIA / NIGERIA	- Nigerian School Library Association - Anambra State School Libraries Association
NORVÈGE / NORWAY	- Skolebibliotekarforeningen i Norge - Norsk Bibliotekforening - Spesialgruppen for bibliotekvirksomhet i skolen (Norwegian Library Association - Section for School Libraries)
NOUVELLE ZÉLANDE / **NEW ZEALAND**	- New Zealand Library and Information Association - School Library Network
OUGANDA / UGANDA	- Uganda Libraries Board - Uganda School Library Association
PAPOUASIE-NOUVELLE GUINÉE / PAPUA NEW GUINEA	- School Library Association
PORTO RICO / PUERTO RICO	- Asociacion de Bibliotecarios Escolares de Puerto Rico
PORTUGAL	- Associaçao Portuguesa de Bibliotecarios, Arquivistas e Documentalistas (BAD) (Groupe de Travail sur les Bibliotheques Scolaires - School Libraries Interest Group)
ROYAUME-UNI / **UNITED KINGDOM**	- The Library Association - School Libraries Group - School Library Association . Scottish Library Group / Library Association - School Libraries Group (Scotland)
SUÈDE / SWEDEN	- Sveriges Allmanna Biblioteksforening (SAB) / Swedish Library Association - Section for School Library Matters
TRINIDAD ET TOBAGO **TRINIDAD AND TOBAGO**	- Library Association of Trinidad and Tobago - School Libraries Group

2.1
ASSOCIATIONS - Liste alphabétique / Alphabetical List
Par / By Paulette Bernhard
Avec la collaboration de :　　　　　　With the collaboration of :
Guylaine Vinet

INTRODUCTION

La liste ci-dessous recense les associations qui se consacrent spécifiquement à la bibliothéconomie scolaire, de même que les sections ou groupes d'intérêt dans ce domaine d'associations plus générales. Elle a été constituée à partir de plusieurs sources dont les plus importantes sont signalées à la fin de cette partie. Étant donné qu'il s'agit d'informations sujettes à des changements fréquents et souvent difficiles à vérifier, nous vous serions très reconnaissants de nous faire part des erreurs et omissions que vous seriez amenés à constater.

The following is an inventory of associations specifically dedicated to school librarianship, as well as of sections and interest groups of broader associations interested in this field. The principal sources used to establish it are cited at the end of this section. Considering that this information is frequently changing and often difficult to verify, we thank you in advance for notifying us of any error or omission that you notice.

INTERNATIONAL

....
Fédération internationale des associations de bibliothécaires et des bibliothèques /
International Federation of Library Associations and Institutions (IFLA)
　　　　URL: http://www.nlc-bnc.ca/ifla/
Section des bibliothèques et centres documentaires scolaires / Section of School
Libraries and Resource Centers
　　　　URL: http://www.nlc-bnc.ca/ifla/VII/s11/ssl.htm
Publ.:　*IFLA Section of School Libraries. Newsletter.*
Contact:　Paulette Bernhard, Chair
　　　　École de bibliothéconomie et des sciences de l'information
　　　　Université de Montréal, C.P. 6128, succursale Centre-ville
　　　　Montréal (Quebec) H3C 3J7　　Canada
　　　　TEL. 514-343-5600　　FAX: 514-343-5753　　　　　　　　　　source: IFLA
....

International Association of School Librarianship (IASL)
Suite 300　　　　P.O. Box 34069
Seattle, Washington 98124-1069　　USA
　　　　TEL.: 604-925 0266　　FAX: 604-925 0566　　E-mail: iasl@rockland.com
　　　　URL: http://www.rhi.hi.is/~anne/linksiasl.html
Publ.:　*International Association of School Librarianship. Newsletter.*
　　　　School libraries worldwide　　　　　　　　　　　　　source: association

---

AFRIQUE DU SUD / SOUTH AFRICA

....
South African School Media Association
c/o Education Media Service, Private Bag X290, Pretoria 0001, South Africa
FAX: 27-12-3227699
Publ.:　*Media Focus = Mediafokus*　　　　　　　　　　　　source: revue

AUSTRALIE / AUSTRALIA
- National

Australian Library and Information Association (ALIA) - School Libraries Section
P.O. Box E441
(ALIA House, 9-11 Napier Close Deakin)
Queen Victoria Terrace, ACT. 2600   Australia
Publ.: *Orana: Australia's national journal of school and children's librarianship*
    TEL.:   61-6 285 1877   FAX: +61-6 282 2249   E-mail: enquiry@alia.org.au
    URL: http://www.alia.org.au   source: page Web

Australian School Library Association (ASLA)
c/o National President
PO Box 450, Belconnen ACT 2616 Australia
President: Karen Bonanno, Queensland Library And Information Services, PO Box 255
Moranbah Queensland 4744 Australia
Publ.:   *Access. Australian School Library Association*
    TEL.: 079 418 045   FAX: 079 418 065
    E-mail: kbonanno@r130.aone.net.au   source: association + page Web

- Régions / Regional

Australian Capital Territory
Australian School Library Association (ACT)
PO Box 25, Griffith ACT 2603   Australia   source: association

New South Wales
Australian School Library Association (NSW)
PO Box 1336, Parramatta NSW 2124   Australia
Publ.: *Teacher and Librarian*   source: association

Northern Territory
School Library Association of Northern Territory
PO Box 3162, Darwin NT 0801   Australia   source: IASL

Queensland
School Library Association of Queensland (SLAQ)
PO Box 997, Toowong, Queensland 4069   Australia
West Perth WA 6872 Australia   source: IASL

South Australia
South Australia School Library Association (SASLA)
PO Box 2093, Kent Town SA 5071   Australia
    URL: http://va.com.au/teaching/slasa/index.html   source: page Web

Tasmania
Australian School Library Association (TAS)
C/- Secretary, Ms Edna Driscoll
Springfield Gardens Primary School, Ashbourne Crescent
West Moonah TAS 7009   Australia   source: association

Victoria
School Library Association of Victoria (SLAV)
217, Church Street, Richmond 3121 Australia
    Tel. 61 03- 94284173 FAX: 61 3 94271329
    E-mail: slav@netspace.net.au
    URL: http://www.srl.rmit.edu.au/slav   source: documents + page Web

Western Australia
Western Australia School Library Association
PO Box 1272

BOTSWANA

Botswana Library Association - Group for School Libraries
Ms Fran Lamuse
P.O. Box 1310 Gaborone   Botswana   source: association

BRÉSIL / BRAZIL

Federaçao Brasileira de Associaoes de Bibliotecarios
Rua Avanhandava 40-conj. 110
Sao Paulo SP 01306 Brazil
  TEL.: 55-11 257 99 79 FAX: 55-11 283 07 47   source: Connections

CANADA
- National

Association for Media and Technology in Education in Canada (AMTEC)
3-1750 The Queensway, Suite 1318
Etobicoke, On M9C 5H5   Canada
  URL: http://www.camosun.bc.ca/~amtec/   source: page Web

Association for Teacher-Librarianship in Canada (ATLC)
782, Warwick Street
Woodstock On   N4S 4R1   Canada
Publ.: *Impact*
  FAX: 519-539-7226
  URL: http://calvin.stemnet.nf.ca/~gnoel/lrc4b.html
Executive Assistant: Angela Thacker E-mail: athacker@istar.ca source: association

Canadian School Library Association (CSLA) - A Division of the Canadian Library Association
200, Elgin Street, Suite 602
Ottawa, On K2P 1L5
Publ. *School Libraries in Canada*
  TEL.: 613-232-9625   FAX: 603-563-9895
  URL: http://www.inforamp.net/~abrown/csla.htm   source: association + page Web

- Provinces / Provinces

Alberta   Alberta Learning Resources Council
c/o 256 Woodhaven Place SW, Calgary, AB   T2W 5 P9   source: page Web CSLA

British Columbia   British Columbia Teacher-Librarians' Association (BCTLA)
c/o B.C. Teacher's Federation, 100-550 West Sixth Avenue
Vancouver, BC V5Z 4P2
Publ.: *Bookmark*
  TEL.: 604-871-2283 ou 800-663-9163
  URL: http://www.inforamp.net/~abrown   source: ATLC + page Web

Manitoba   Manitoba School Library Association (MSLA)
c/o Manitoba Teacher's Society, President: Michelle Larose-Kuzenko
191 Harcourt St., Winnipeg MB H3J 3H2   Canada   E-mail: mlarose@minet.gov.mb.ca
  URL: http://www.mbnet.mb.ca/~msla   source: page Web CSLA

New Brunswick   Library Council of the New Brunswick Teachers Association
P.O. Box 752
Fredericton, NB E3B 5R6   Canada   source: page Web CSLA
Note: dissolution to come in June 1997   source: *Impact*

Newfoundland Newfoundland Learning Resources Council
President: Gary Noel, 604 Topsail Road
St. Johns NF   A1E 2C9   Canada   source: page Web CSLA

North West Territories NWTTALRC
President: Michell Krause
6, Perkins Court
Yellowknife NWT X1A 3L7   Canada   source: page Web CSLA

Nova Scotia   Nova Scotia School Library Association (NSSLA)
Florence O'Neill c/o NSTU
3105 Dutch Village Road
Halifax NS   Canada   source: *Impact*

Ontario   Ontario School Library Association (OSLA)
c/o Liz Kerr, President
100 Lombard St., Suite 303
Toronto, On   M5C 1M3 Canada   source: page Web CSLA

Prince Edward Island   P.E.I. Teacher-Librarian's Association (PEITLA)
c/o Federation House, PO Box 600
Charlottetown, P.E.I. C1A 8B4   Canada   source: page Web CSLA

Québec
- Association du personnel des services documentaires scolaires (APSDS)
     URL: http://rtsq.grics.qc.ca/apsds/
     Secrétaire: André Bigras, 127, rue Pilon, Saint-Eustache, Qué J7P 2J5 Canada
     Président: Yvon Joubert TEL.:: 514-467-0262   FAX: 514-466-4295   source: association

- Quebec Library Association - School Libraries Section
  President: Rennie McLeod
  525, Pleasant Avenue, Westmount, Qué H3Y 3H6 Canada   source: page Web CSLA

Saskatchewan
- Saskatchewan School Library Association (SSLA)
  c/o Meradith Churchill, Box 285
  Regina Beach SK S0G 4C0   Canada   source: *Impact*

- Saskatchewan Library Association
  President: Ellen Bechard
  Saskatchewan Teachers Federation
  Mooe Jaw SK S6H 3V8   Canada   source: page Web CSLA

- Yukon   Yukon LTA
  c/o Eleanor Donovan
  2065, 2nd St., Whitehorse, Yukon Territory Y1C 2C6   source: page Web CSLA

CHILI / CHILE

Association for School and Public Librarians
Publ.: *ABIEP. Boletin (Boletin-Chile)*   source: contact IFLA

CROATIE / CROATIA

Croatian Library Association - Committee for School Libraries
Marulicev Trg 21
Zagreb YU-41000 Croatia
Publ.: *Bulletin of School Librarians*
    TEL. and FAX: 385-41 440 846   source: *Connections*

DANEMARK / DENMARK

Danmarks Skolebiblioteksforening / Danish School Library Association
Vesterbrogade 20
DK 1620, Copenhagen V   Denmark
Publ.: *Boern og Boeger, Skolebiblioteksåarbog (School Library annual))*
    TEL.: 45-33 25 32 22   FAX: 45-33 25 32 23
    E-mail: KomSkolBib@internet.dk   source: association

Danmarks Skolebibliotekarforening / Association of Danish School Librarians
Chairman: Gert Larsen, School Library Adviser
Gogevej 2, POB 1
4130 Viby Zealand
Publ.: *Skolebiblioteket (The School Library)*
    TEL.: 45-46 19 34 40   FAX: 45-46 19 43 49   source: document

ÉGYPTE / EGYPT

Egyptian School Library Association
35 al-Galaa St., Cairo, Egypt
TEL.: 753 001
Publ.: *Sahifat al-Maktabat (Library Journal)*   source: *Connections* + vérif.

ESPAGNE / SPAIN

Associacion Educacion y Biblioteca
Madrid : TILDE Servicios Editoriales S.A., en colaboracion con
Baeza, 4, Oficina 4, 28002 Madrid
Publ.: *Educacion y Biblioteca. Revista mensual de decumentacion y recusos didacticos.*
TEL.: 415 17 50 ; 519 38 78   source: revue

ÉTATS-UNIS d'AMÉRIQUE / UNITED STATES OF AMERICA
- National

American Association of School Librarians (AASL) - A division of the American Library Association
50 East Huron Street, Chicago IL 60611-2795   USA
Publ.: *School Library Media Quarterly*
TEL.: 800-545-2433, ext: 4381   312-280-4381   FAX: 312-664-7459
    URL: http://www.ala.org/aasl/index.html   source: association + page Web

Association for Educational Communications and Technology (AECT)
Division of School Media Specialists (DSMS)
c/0 Helen M. Wing, President, Lloyd C. Bird High School
3111 E. Weyburn Road, Richmond, VA 23235 USA
    TEL.: 804-768-6110   FAX: 804-768-6117
    URL: http://www.aect.org   source: association + page Web

ÉTATS-UNIS d'AMÉRIQUE / UNITED STATES OF AMERICA
- États / States

Pour les sections de l'AASL et de l'AECT, voir / For the AASL and AECT Sections see :
"List of State Associations with Affiliates." *School library media annual*, vol. 12, 1994,
pp. 286-287, et les sites Web des deux associations / and the Web sites of both associations.

ÉTHIOPIE / ETHIOPIA

Committee for the Development of School-Community Library for Children
P.O. Box 25 196   Addis Ababa   Ethiopia   source: association

FRANCE

Centre d'étude de la documentation et de l'information scolaires (CEDIS)
2, résidence de Guinette, 91150 Étampes, France
     TEL.: 33- 1-64-94-39-51   FAX: 33-1-64-94-49-35
Publ.:   *Inter BCD   Revue des bibliothèques centres documentaires*
     Inter CDI. Revue des centres de documentation et d'information scolaires   source: revues

Fédération des Enseignants Documentalistes de l'Éducation nationale (FADBEN)
B.P. 129   75 223 Paris Cédex 05 France
Publ.: *Médiadoc*
     TEL. et FAX : 33- 1-43 72 45 60
France Vernotte, présidente   TEL. et FAX: 3-81 58 88 98   source: association

GHANA

Ghana Library Association - Ghana School Library Association
P.O. Box 663   Accra, Ghana
     TEL.: 233-21 665 083   source: *Connections*

HONG KONG

Hong Kong Teacher-Librarians' Association
Flat C, 11/F, 7 Broadway, Mei Foo Sun Chuen,
Kowloon, Hong Kong
     FAX: 852-2741 5039   E-mail: mmhung@hkein.school.net.hk
     URL: http://hkein.school.net.hk/~mmhung/hktla.htm   source: page Web

HONGRIE / HUNGARY

Hungarian Teacher Librarian Association
c/o Zsuzsanna Celler, National Educational Library & Museum
P.O. Box 49
Budapest H1363   Hungary   source: IASL

ILES FIDJI / FIJI ISLANDS

Fiji Library Association - School Libraries Interest Group
PO Box 1168, Suva   Fiji   source: association

INDE / INDIA

Indian Library Association - Central Sectional Committee for School Libraries
P.O. Box 663
Accra, Ghana   TEL.: 233-21 665 083   source: *Connections*

INDONÉSIE / INDONESIA

Majala IPI. School Library Division
Jakarta: Ikatan Pustakawan Indonesia.
Publ.: *Majalah IPI. School Library Division*   source: revue

ITALIE / ITALY

Ente Nazionale per la Biblioteche Poplari e Scolastiche (National Group for Public and School
Libraries)
c/0 Via Michele Mercati 4
Roma Italy
Publ.: *Le Parola e il Libro* (*The Word and the Book*)   Source: *Connections*

JAMAÏQUE / JAMAICA

Jamaica Library Association (JLA) - Schools Section
PO Box 58
Kigston 5   Jamaica
        URL: http://www.jol.com.jm/thelwelr/jla.html   source: association + page Web

JAPON / JAPAN

Japan School Library Association
Secretary: Ms R. Sakagawa
2-7 Kasuka 2-chome
Bunkyo-ku
Tokyo 112   Japan
Publ.: *Gakkou Toshokan Sokuhoban*   sources: association + contact IFLA

MALAISIE / MALAYSIA

Library Association of Malaysia - School Library Committee
c/o National Library of Malaysia
232 Jalan Tun Razak,
50572 Kuala Lumpur,Malaysia
President of the Committee: Diljit Singh E-mail: diljit@fsktm.um.edu.my   source: committee

Malaysian Educational Technology Association
c/o Centre for Educational Technology and Media
Science University of Malaysia, Minden,
11800 Penang Malaysia
President: Dr. Abdul Rahim Saad E-mail is arms@usm.my   source: contact IASL

NIGÉRIA / NIGERIA

Nigerian School Library Association
Medical Residence, University of Ibadan
Ibadan   Nigeria
Publ.:   *Nigerian School Library Journal*
          Nigerian School Library Association. Newsletter   source: *Connections*

- États / States

Anambra State School Libraries Association
c/o Enugu Campus Library, University of Nigeria, Enugu, Nigeria
Publ.: *School Libraries Bulletin*   source: revue

NORVÈGE / NORWAY

Skolebibliotekarforeningen i Norge
v/Ragnhild Mydland, Pramvn. 14, 4624 Kristiansand Norway
Addr.for Newsletter: Baldersvein 7, 7600 Levanger Norway TEL.: 38 08 60 25   source: contact IFLA

Norsk Bibliotekforening - Spesialgruppen for bibliotekvirksomhet i skolen
(Norwegian Library Association - Section for School Libraries)
Malerhaugveien 20, N-0661 Oslo   Norway
TEL.: 22 68 85 50   FAX: 22 67 23 68
URL: http://www.sn.no/~keielsen   source: contact + page Web

NOUVELLE-ZÉLANDE / NEW ZEALAND

New Zealand Library and Information Association - School Library Network
PO Box 12-212   Wellington New Zealand
TEL.: 64-4 473 58 34 FAX: 64-4 499 14 80
URL: http://www.netlink.co.nz/~nzlia/   source: association + page Web

OUGANDA / UGANDA

Uganda Libraries Board - Uganda School Library Association
c/o Public Libraries Board, Bugunda Road, P.O. Box 4262
Kampala, Uganda   source: *Connections*

PAPOUASIE-NOUVELLE GUINÉE / PAPUA NEW GUINEA

School Library Association
J.A. Evans, SPCenCIID, P.O. Box 320, University PO
Papua New Guinea   source: IASL
Publ.: *Newsletter*

PORTO RICO / PUERTO RICO

Asociacion de Bibliotecarios Escolares de Puerto Rico
P.O. Box 19 1559 San Juan 00919-1559
Puerto Rico   source: association

PORTUGAL

Associaçao Portuguesa de Bibliotecarios, Arquivistas e Documentalistas (BAD)
(Groupe de Travail sur les Bibliotheques Scolaires - School Libraries Interest Group)
R. Morais Soares 43C-1° DTO
1900 Lisboa   Portugal
TEL.: 351-1 815 44 79   FAX: 351-1 815 45 08   source: association

ROYAUME-UNI / UNITED KINGDOM

The Library Association - School Libraries Group
7, Ridgmount Street, London WC1E 7AE   England   (group: 148 Annandale Road, London SE10 OJZ)
Publ.: *School Libraries in view*   source: association + page Web
TEL.: 71-636 7543   FAX: 71-436 7218   URL: http://www.la-hq.org.uk/slg.htm

School Library Association
c/o Ms Valerie Fea, Executive Secretary, Liden Library, Barrington Close, Liden
Swindon, Wiltshire SN3 6HF   United Kingdom
Publ.: *School Librarian*
TEL.: 44-793 61 78 38   source: association

- Scotland

Scottish Library Group / Library Association - School Libraries Group
Secretary : Krista Ranson, Westhill Academy Library,
Grampian Regional Council, Schools Library Service   source: page Web
Hay's Way, Westhill   AB3 6XZ   UK Scotland   TEL.: 41-224 74 01 11
URL: http://www.almac.co.uk/business_park/slainte/slainte2/slainteg/2schlig0.html

SUÈDE / SWEDEN

Allmanna Biblioteksforening (SAB) / Swedish Library Association - Section for School Library Matters /
Helle Barrett, Malneo SBC, Hardovag 5 S-21367 Malneo Sweden   source: association + contact IFLA

TRINIDAD ET TOBAGO / TRINIDAD AND TOBAGO

Library Association of Trinidad and Tobago - School Libraries Group
P.O. Box 1275, Port of Spain, Trinidd and Tobago
Publ.: *Newsletter of the School Libraries Group*   Source: *Connections*

Sources consultées / Sources consulted

- International Federation of Library Associations and Institutions (IFLA). Secretariat. Addresses of members of the Section of School Libraries and Resource Centers, 1996 + 1997.
- International Association of School Librarianship. *Worldwide directory: a listing of personal, institutional and association members.* 1996. Seattle, WA: IASL, 1996. 82 p.
- Oberg, Dianne; Steward, Keye (Comp.). *Connections: School Library Associations and Contact people Worldwide.* Kalamazoo, MI: International Association of School Librarianship, 1994. 96 p.
- "List of State Associations with Affiliates." *School library media annual,* vol. 12, 1994, pp. 286-287.
  (Note: list of AASL and AECT sections, US / Liste des sections de l'AASL et de l'AECT, États-Unis)

Pages Web pointant vers des associations / Web pages linking to associations :
- Canadian School Library Association (CSLA). May 20, 1997. (On line) URL address:
  http://www.inforamp.net/~abrown/csla.htm
- International Federation of Library Associations and Institutions (IFLA). May 6-17, 1997. (On line)
  URL address: **http://www.nlc-bnc.ca/ifla/**
- *K-12 School Librarian Professional Association Pages.* May 20, 1997. (On line) URL address:
  http://www.cusd.chico.k12.ca.us/~pmilbury/pro.html

2.2

**PRINCIPALES LISTES DE DISCUSSION À L'INTENTION DES RESPONSABLES
DE BIBLIOTHÈQUES ET DE CENTRES DOCUMENTAIRES SCOLAIRES**

**PRINCIPAL LISTSERVS FOR THOSE RESPONSIBLE
FOR SCHOOL LIBRARIES AND RESOURCE CENTERS**

Par / By Paulette Bernhard

INTRODUCTION

On trouvera ci-dessous la mention des principales listes de discussion destinées aux bibliothécaires et aux enseignants-documentalistes du milieu scolaire, ainsi que quelques sources permettant d'identifier d'autres listes d'intérêt. Bien que très jeunes, ces listes représentent un moyen de communication extrêmement prisé par les reponsables des bibliothèques et des centres documentaires des établissements scolaires, souvent isolés dans leurs institutions. La doyenne de ces listes, LM_NET, compte plus de 7600 abonnés et leur nombre ne cesse de croître! Pour chaque liste, nous avons indiqué le pays où elle est hébergée, l'année de création et le nombre d'abonnés, lorsque disponible.

Un certain nombre d'explications générales sur le fonctionnement des listes de discussion sont disponibles sur le site Web de l'IFLA à l'adresse URL: **http://www.nlc-bnc.ca/ifla/II/iflalist.htm**

The principal listservs devoted to school librarians and teacher librarians are presented in the following pages, as well as some sources which can help to find other interesting lists. Although they are in an early stage, these lists represent a very powerful communications tool between those responsible for school libraries and resource centres, who are often isolated in their institutions. LM_NET, the first of the school libraries listservs, has more than 7600 subscribers, a number that keeps growing! For each list, we indicate the country where it is located, the year it was created and, when available, the number of subscribers.

Some general explanations about how listservs function can be found on the IFLA Web site at the following URL address: **http://www.nlc-bnc.ca/ifla/II/iflalist.htm**

LISTES FRANCOPHONES

CDIDOC (France) 1996-   **292 abonnés (juin 1997)**

Liste ouverte aux documentalistes et enseignants de disciplines des établissements scolaires des pays francophones. Thèmes et sujets de débats: la pédagogie documentaire; le documentaliste dans l'équipe pédagogique; le travail en réseau des documentalistes; Internet et le multimédia au centre de documentation et d'information; l'évolution du métier de documentaliste en établissement scolaire; échanges d'informations professionnelles.

Lists aimed at teacher librarians (documentalists) and teachers in schools of French speaking countries. Topics of discussion: resource-based pedagogy, the teacher-librarian as part of the educational team, working in networks, Internet and multimedia at the school library/resource center, evolution of the profession of teacher librarian, exchange of professional information.

- adresse du serveur / mail to : **listserv@univ-rennes1.fr**
- dans la ligne "sujet" écrire uniquement / in 'subject' line, write only : **subscribe cdidoc-fr**
- ne RIEN mettre dans le message (effacer toute autre note/adresse) / NOTHING in the message (cancel any note/address)
- adresse à laquelle envoyer des messages aux membres de la liste pour participer aux discussions / for participating to the discussions, messages should be sent to : **cdidoc-fr@univ-rennes1.fr**

- Web: *CDIDOC*. Adresse URL : **http://www.cru.fr/listes/cdidoc-fr@cru.fr/**
       Archives de la liste. Adresse URL: **http://www.univ-rennes1.fr/LISTES/cdidoc-fr@univ-rennes1.fr/archives/tous.html**

MODÉRATEURS / MODERATORS : Marie-Hélène Pillon et Claude Hellot, Centre Régional de Documentation Pédagogique de Bretagne, Moderateur.cdidoc-fr@univ-rennes1.fr

EDUDOC (Belgique / Belgium) 1995-   **Environ 300 abonnés (mai 1997)**
Liste de discussion sur la formation des utilisateurs des bibliothèques et centres de documentation.

Mise sur pied et gérée par le "Groupe Formation des Utilisateurs" des bibliothèques et centres de documentation de l'Association Belge de Documentation, cette liste de discussion est consacrée à la "didactique de l'accès à l'information et de l'exploitation des ressources documentaires". Les objectifs visent à permettre l'échange de savoir faire, de matériel pédagogique, d'idées nouvelles et de toute autre information.

This listserv, created and managed by the "Bibliographic Instruction Group" of the Belgian Association of Documentation, is devoted to instruction on how to access information and to use documentary resources. The objectives are the exchange of know-how, pedagogic material, new ideas and any other information.

- adresse du serveur / mail to : **LISTSERV@VM1.ULG.AC.BE**
- ne rien inscrire dans la ligne "subject" / leave 'subject' blank
- dans le message, écrire uniquement / in the message, write only the following :
         subscribe edudoc nom, prénom, institution
         subscribe edudoc family name, first name, institution
- adresse à laquelle envoyer des messages aux membres de la liste pour participer aux discussions / for participating to the discussions, messages should be sent to : **EDUDOC@vm1.ulg.ac.be**

RESPONSABILITÉ / RESPONSIBILITY : Paul Thirion, pthirion@vm1.ulg.ac.be
                                         Francoise Noël, fnoel@vm1.ulg.ac.be

LISTSERVS IN ENGLISH

ATLC Forum (Canada) 1995–
Association for Teacher Librarianship in Canada (ATLC)
182 subscribers (June 1997)

This Forum is a membership service of the Association for Teacher-Librarianship in Canada (ATLC). Its purpose is to provide members with the opportunity to share information and viewpoints, as well as to ask (and answer!) questions of interest to other members.

Liste de discussion destinée aux membres de l'Association for Teacher-Librarianship in Canada (ATLC) en vue de leur permettre d'échanger des informations et des points de vue, ainsi que de poser des questions d'intérêt général à la communauté (et d'y répondre!).

- adresse du serveur / mail to : **mailserv@camosun.bc.ca**
- ne rien inscrire dans la ligne "subject" / leave 'subject' blank
- dans le message, écrire uniquement / in the message, write only the following :
    SUBSCRIBE ATLC prénom nom / SUBSCRIBE ATLC first name family name
- adresse à laquelle envoyer des messages aux membres de la liste pour participer aux discussions / for participating to the discussions, messages should be sent to : **atlcforum@camosun.bc.ca**

RESPONSABILITÉ / RESPONSIBILITY : Angela Thacker, athacker@istar.ca

BIGSIX (États-Unis) 1995–
Big Six approach to information literacy
1,446 subscribers (May 1997)

The BigSix listserv was started in January 1995 to facilitate communication between users of the Big Six Information Problem-Solving Model. Subscribers of this discussion group range from beginners to experienced users of the Big Six.

Liste de discussion axée sur la formation à la maîtrise de l'information au primaire et au secondaire. Dédiée aux utilisateurs du modèle de résolution de problèmes informationnels en six étapes élaboré par Mike Eisenberg et Robert E. Berkowitz.

- serveur : **LISTSERV@LISTSERV.SYR.EDU**
- ne rien inscrire dans la ligne "subject" / leave 'subject' blank
- dans le message, écrire uniquement / in the message, write only the following :
    subscribe BigSix prénom nom / subscribe BigSix first name family name
- adresse à laquelle envoyer des messages aux membres de la liste pour participer aux discussions / for participating to the discussions, messages should be sent to : **bigsix@listserv.syr.edu**

- Web : *The Big Six Skills© Information Problem-Solving Approach to Library and Information Skills Instruction.* URL address: **http://ericir.syr.edu/big6/bigsix.html**
    BigSix Listserv Archives. URL address: **http://ericir.syr.edu/big6/bigsix.html**

RESPONSABILITÉ / RESPONSIBILITY : Mike Eisenberg, mike@ericir.syr.edu
Bob Berkowitz, reberkow@MAILBOX.SYR.EDU

IASL-LINK (International) 1995–
International Association of School Librarianship (IASL)
About 100 subscribers (May 1997)

IASL-LINK is for communication between members of the Association throughout the world, and for the distribution of announcements, discussion papers, articles, news, information about projects, and information from IASL conferences and meetings.

Cette liste se veut un moyen de communication à travers le monde entre les membres de l'association et sert à la diffusion d'annonces, de textes soumis à discussion, d'articles, d'informations relatives à des projets et de comptes rendus des congrès et rencontres de l'IASL.

IASL-LINK (continued)

- adresse du serveur / mail to : **majordomo@rhi.hi.is**
- ne rien inscrire dans la ligne "subject" / leave 'subject' blank
- dans le message, écrire uniquement / in the message, write only the following :
  subscribe iasl-link votre adesse électronique
  subscribe iasl-link your e-mail address
- adresse à laquelle envoyer des messages aux membres de la liste pour participer aux discussions / for participating to the discussions, messages should be sent to : **iasl-link@rhi.hi.is**

RESPONSABILITÉ / RESPONSIBILITY: Anne Clyde, anne@rhi.hi.is

....

InfoLit_Aust (Australie / Australia) 1996-   **244 subscribers (May 1997)**
A National Listserv for Information Literacy Collaboration for Primary, Secondary and Tertiary Education Sectors

Dealing specifically with information literacy issues, this electronic forum is intended to bring together all parties interested and involved in developing information literacy programs in the primary, secondary and post-compulsory education sectors. It is a service uniquely designed to foster interaction and collaboration between these different education sectors in developing information literate students to become independent and lifelong learners.

Spécialement consacrée à la problématique de la culture de l'information, cette liste a pour objectif de rassembler toutes les personnes intéressées et préoccupées par la mise en place de programmes de formation à la maîtrise de l'information dans les secteurs éducatifs du primaire, du secondaire et de l'éducation des adultes. Il s'agit d'un service spécialement conçu pour susciter interaction et collaboration entre ces différents secteurs, en vue de former des apprenants capables de faire usage de l'information de façon indépendante tout au long de leur vie.

- adresse du serveur / mail to : **InfoLit_Aust-request@listserv.csu.edu.au**
- dans la ligne "sujet" écrire uniquement / in 'subject' line, write only :   **subscribe**
- ne RIEN mettre dans le message (enlever votre adresse automatique, le cas échéant) / NOTHING in the message (cancel any note/address)
- les nouveaux abonnés sont invités à se présenter lors de l'envoi de leur premier message / new subscribers are encouraged to introduce themselves in their first message to the listserv.
- adresse à laquelle envoyer des messages aux membres de la liste pour participer aux discussions / for participating to the discussions, messages should be sent to :
  InfoLit_Aust@listserv.csu.edu.au

Administrators / Administrateurs :   Lyn Hay, lhay@csu.edu.au
                                            Irene Doskatsch, Irene.Doskatsch@unisa.edu.au

....

LM_NET (États-Unis) 1992-   **7,667 subscribers (May 1997)**
School Library Media and Network Communications

LM_NET (Library Media Net). LM_NET is open to all school library media specialists worldwide and others who have an interest in this field. The main topics of discussion are: Internet Resources, Library Administration, CDROM (especially encyclopedias), Other Media and In print resources and the role of the media specialist.

LM_NET s'adresse aux bibliothécaires et enseignants-documentalistes en milieu scolaire à travers le monde, ainsi qu'à tous ceux qui s'intéressent à ce domaine. Ses principaux domaines d'intérêt sont: les ressources de l'Internet; la gestion de la bibliothèque; les DOCs (disques optiques numériques), en particulier les encyclopédies; les autres ressources audiovisuelles et imprimées; le rôle du spécia-liste des média en milieu scolaire.

LM_NET (continued)

- serveur : **LISTSERV@LISTSERV.SYR.EDU**
- ne rien inscrire dans la ligne "subject" / leave 'subject' blank
- dans le message, écrire uniquement / in the message, write only the following :
  subscribe lm_net prenom nom
  subscribe lm_net first name family name
- adresse à laquelle envoyer des messages aux membres de la liste pour participer aux discussions /
  for participating to the discussions, messages should be sent to :
  LM_NET@LISTSERV.SYR.EDU

- Web : *Welcome to LM_NET On the World Wide Web!*   URL : http://ericir.syr.edu/lm_net/

RESPONSABILITÉ / RESPONSIBILITY :   Mike Eisenberg, mike@ericir.syr.edu
Peter Milbury, pmilbur@eis.calstate.edu

....

OZTL_NET (Australie) 1995-   **1303 subscribers (May 1997)**
The Australian teacher librarians' listserv

OZTL_NET stands for OZ(Aus)tralian Teacher Librarians' NET-work. This electronic forum is intended to be an effective management tool for practising TLs. Discussion on OZTL_NET may include: library, school and departmental policies, practices and procedures; location and use of Internet resources; information literacy issues, programs and strategies; reference questions for teachers and students; products and services for school libraries; general discussion of teacher librarianship issues; training tips and use of information technologies; and workshop and conference announcements.

Il s'agit du réseau australien des enseignants-documentalistes. Cette liste de discusson a pour objectif de servir de moyen efficace de gestion pour les professionnels en place. Les thèmes susceptibles d'être abordés sont les suivants: politiques et règlements de la bibliothèque, de l'école et du regroupe-ment; pratiques et règles de procédure; programmes et stratégies; questions de référence à l'inten-tion des enseignants et des élèves; produits et services pour les bibliothèques scolaires; discussions générales en matière de bibliothéconomie scolaire; bonnes idées sur la formation et sur l'utilisation des technologies de l'information; annonces d'ateliers et de conférences.

- adresse du serveur / mail to : **OZTL_NET-request@listserv.csu.edu.au**
- dans la ligne "sujet" écrire uniquement / in 'subject' line, write only :   **subscribe**
- ne RIEN mettre dans le message (enlever votre adresse automatique, le cas échéant) / NOTHING in the message (cancel any note/address)
- adresse à laquelle envoyer des messages aux membres de la liste pour participer aux discussions / for participating to the discussions, messages should be sent to :
  OZTL_NET@listserv.csu.edu.au
- les nouveaux abonnés sont invités à se présenter lors de l'envoi de leur premier message /new subscribers are encouraged to introduce themselves in their first message to the listserv.

ADMINISTRATEURS / ADMINISTRATORS :   Lyn Hay, lhay@csu.edu.au
Ken Dillon, kdillon@csu.edu.au
~~~~~~

POUR TROUVER D'AUTRES LISTES DE DISCUSSION / FINDING OTHER LISTSERVS

....

» RÉPERTOIRES SPÉCIALISÉS / SPECIALIZED DIRECTORIES
....

- Bernhard, Paulette. *Formation à la maîtrise de l'information: une sélection d'outils à l'intention des formateurs.* (En ligne) Adresse URL:
  http://tornade.ere.umontreal.ca/~bernh/AAFD.97/AAFD.index

48

» RÉPERTOIRES SPÉCIALISÉS / SPECIALIZED DIRECTORIES (continued)

- Clyde, Laurel A. *School librarianship listservs: a list of listservs for school librarians created in 1995 for members of the Association's IASL-LINK listserv.* (On line) URL address : **http://www.rhi.hi.is/~anne/listservs.html**

> Other lists cited:
> **BooKBraG** ("the best new children's books and the brightest ideas for using them in your classroom"), **KIDLIT-L** (discussing children's literature), **CHILDLIT** (an alternative to the KIDLIT-L listserv with emphasis on discussion of "criticism and theory", **OZ-TEACHERS** for all "Australian teachers and their colleagues"), **PUBYAC** (discussion of "library services to children and young adults in public libraries"), **EDTECH** (all aspects of technology and its use in education), **IFREEDOM** (Canadian listserv dealing with intellectual freedom, censorship issues, and problems arising from challenges to library materials), **SIRSNET** ("enables SIRS customers and prospective customers to share information and ideas with one another about SIRS and its products").

- *IFLANET mailing lists.* URL address: **http://www.nlc-bnc.ca/ifla/ll/iflalist.htm**
Aussi disponible sur CD-ROM: *IFLANET Unplugged*. La Haye : IFLA and SilverPlatter International, 1996.

> **IFLA-L** (Forum intended to foster communications between IFLA, its membership and members of the international library community. The goal in establishing this list is to facilitate information exchange as well as professional communication and development within the IFLA community);
> **DIGLIB** (for librarians, information scientists, and other information professionals to discuss the constellation of issues and technologies pertaining to the creation of digital libraries);
> **LIBJOBS** (for librarians and information professionals seeking employment. Subscribers receive only job postings).

- *Internet Learning Resources. Directory.* (United Kingdom / Royaume Uni) (On line) URL address:
http://www.rgu.ac.uk/~sim/research/netlearn/callist.htm

....

» RÉPERTOIRES DE LISTES / LISTSERV DIRECTORIES
....

- *Francopholistes.* (En ligne) Adresse URL: **http://www.cru.fr/listes/**

- *CataList, the official catalog of LISTSERV® lists : 12,958 public lists out of 46,967 LISTSERV lists .* (30 May, 1997) (On line) URL adress: **http://www.lsoft.com/lists/listref.html**

Troisième partie / Part Three

~~~
# Revues en bibliothéconomie scolaire
~~~
Periodicals in School Librarianship
~~~

Avec la collaboration de :　　　　With the Collaboration of :
Colette Charrier, Niels Jacobsen, Lyn Hay, Teruyo Horikawa,
Torny Kjekstad, Benoit Létourneau, Richard Morin,
Robert Roy, Guylaine Vinet

Nous remercions les personnes suivantes
qui ont particulièrement contribué à cette partie :

We thank the following persons
who have greatly contributed to this part :

- élaboration de la liste initiale / creation of initial list
Niels Jacobsen

- vérifications / verification
Robert Roy

- édition et index / editing and index
Benoit Létourneau

- correction et révision / correction and revision
Colette Charrier, Lyn Hay, Teruyo Horikawa,
Niels Jacobsen, Torny Kjekstad, Glenys Willars

3.1

REVUES EN BIBLIOTHÉCONOMIE SCOLAIRE
Liste alphabétique

PERIODICALS IN SCHOOL LIBRARIANSHIP
Alphabetical List of Titles

Avec la collaboration de :   With the collaboration of :

Niels Jacobsen, Benoit Létourneau, Richard Morin, Robert Roy et Guylaine Vinet

INTRODUCTION

On trouvera dans la partie qui suit le signalement de cinquante-cinq revues et bulletins en bibliothéconomie scolaire qui existent à travers le monde. Cette liste comprend les revues des associations et organismes nationaux et internationaux, ainsi que les bulletins internes des associations et organismes qui ne publient pas de revue. Elle ne comprend pas les revues et bulletins des associations et organismes des états, provinces ou autres regroupements internes à un pays.

La liste initiale a été élaborée par Niels Jacobsen puis révisée et mise à jour grâce à la collaboration des membres du bureau de la Section des bibliothèques scolaires et des personnes-ressources qui ont accepté de la revoir. Nous les remercions chaleureusement pour leur participation.

L'information concernant les périodiques étant sujette à de fréquentes modifications, nous vous serons très reconnaissants de nous faire part des erreurs et omissions que vous constaterez, ainsi que des nouveaux titres dont vous aurez connaissance.

The following pages present fifty five journals and newsletters in school librarianship existing around the world. This list contains journals published by national and international associations and organizations as well as newsletters of the ones that do not publish a journal. It does not contain journals and newsletters from associations and organizations of state, provincial or other divisions internal to a country.

The initial list has been prepared by Niels Jacobsen and was later corrected and updated with the collaboration of the members of the Standing Committee of the Section of School Libraries and the resource persons who have agreed to revise it. We thank them warmly for their collaboration.

As the information about periodicals is subject to frequent changes, we thank you for notifying us of any errors and omissions that you notice, as well as for communicating to us the references of new titles you are aware of.

ABIEP. Boletin (Chili / Chile)
Chile: Association for School and Public Librarians, 1985-
ISSN: 0717-022X
FREQUENCY: 2 per yr.

Access. Australian School Library Association (Australie / Australia)
Elizabeth: Australian School Library Association, 1964-
ISSN: 1030-0155
FREQUENCY: Quarterly
ADDRESS: 480 E. Wilson Bridge Rd., Ste L. Worthington OH 43085
Supersedes (in 1987): Australian School Librarian: ISSN 0005-0199

Les actes de lecture (France)
Paris: Association francaise pour la lecture, 1983-
ISSN: 0758-1475
FREQUENCY: 4 per yr.

Argos: revue des B C D et des C D I (France)
Le Perreux: Centre Régional de Documentation Pédagogique (Créteil), 1989-
ISSN: 0995-2187
FREQUENCY: 3 per yr.
ADDRESS: 20 rue D. Casanova 94170 Le Perreux, France
TEL.: 33-1-48 72 70 70   FAX: 331-48 72 60 72

Barn och Kultur = Children and Culture (Suède / Sweden)
Lund: Bibliotekstjaenst, 1955-
ISSN: 0037-6477
FREQUENCY: 6 per yr.
ADDRESS: P.O. Box 200, S-221 00 Lund, Sweden
TEL.: 46-18-00-00   FAX: 46-30-79-47
Formerly: *Skolbiblioteket*

Bermuda Association of School Librarians (Bermudes / Bermuda)
A Newsletter, published by the Ministry of Education, issued 3 times a year.

Boern og Boeger (Children and Books) (Danemark / Denmark)
Copenhagen: Danmarks Skolebiblioteksforening (Danish School Library Association), 1948-
Text in Danish; summaries in English
ISSN: 0006-7792
FREQUENCY: 8 per yr.
ADDRESS: Vesterbrogade 20, DK 1620, Copenhagen V   Denmark
TEL.: 45-33 25 32 22   FAX: 45-33 25 32 23

Bookmark (Canada)
Vancouver: British Columbia Teachers' Federation; British Columbia Teacher-Librarians' Association.
ISSN: 0381-6028
FREQUENCY: Quarterly
ADDRESS: 100-550 W. 6th Ave., Vancouver, BC V5Z 4P2 Canada
TEL.: 604-871-1848; 800-663-9163   FAX: 604-871-2291

Book Report: journal for junior and senior high school librarians (États-Unis / United States)
Worthington, OH: Linworth Publishing, 1982-
ISSN: 0731-4388
FREQUENCY: bi-m. (during school yr.)
ADDRESS: 480 E. Wilson Bridge Rd., Ste L. Worthington OH 43085
TEL.: 614-436-7107   FAX: 614-436-9490

Bulletin of School Librarians (Croatie / Croatia)
Croatian Library Association - Committee for School Libraries
Marulicev Trg 21
Zagreb YU-41000 Croatia
TEL. and FAX: 385-41 440 846

Choisir (France)
Paris: Centre National de Documentation Pedagogique, 1995-
ISSN: 1261-0666
FREQUENCY: m. (10 per yr.)
ADDRESS: 29 rue d'Ulm 75230 Paris Cedex 05, France
Remplace *Périoscope* ISSN: 0989-6465

College and Undergraduate Libraries (États-Unis / United States)
Binghamton, NY: Haworth Press, 1994-
ISSN: 1069-1316
FREQUENCY: Semiannual
ADDRESS: 10 Alice St., Birghamton, NY 13904
TEL.: 800-342-9678   FAX: 607-722-1424

Community & Junior College Libraries: the journal for learning resources centers (États-Unis /
United States)   Binghamton, NY: Haworth Press, 1982-
ISSN: 0276-3915
FREQUENCY: Semiannual
ADDRESS: 10 Alice St., Birghamton, NY 13904
TEL.: 607-722-5857; 800-342-9678   FAX: 607-722-1424

Education Librarians Group News (Royaume Uni / United Kingdom)
Edgbaston: Library Association ; Education Librarians Group; The Education Library , University of
Birmingham, 1971-
ISSN: 0267-3641
FREQUENCY: 3 per yr.
ADDRESS: University of Birmingham, Edgbaston, Birmingham, B15 2TT, England
TEL.: 0121-414-4870   FAX: 0121-471-4691
Supersedes (in 1981): C I S E Newsletter

Education Libraries Journal (Royaume Uni / United Kingdom)
Nottingham : Trent University, 1958-
ISSN: 0957-9575
FREQUENCY: 3 per yr.
ADDRESS: Trent University, Clifton, Nottingham NG11 8NS, England
TEL.: 0115 94184818 Extn. 3421   FAX: 0115 9486304
Formerly: *Education Libraries Bulletin*   ISSN 0013-1407

Educacion y Biblioteca. Revista mensual de documentacion y recusos didacticos. (Espagne /
Spain)   Madrid : TILDE Servicios Editoriales S.A., en colaboracion con Associacion Educacion y
Biblioteca, 1989-
ISSN: 0214-7491
FREQUENCY: Monthly
ADDRESS: Baeza, 4, Oficina 4, 28002 Madrid   TEL.: 415 17 50 ; 519 38 78

Emergency librarian (Canada)
Vancouver, B.C., Ken Haycock and Associates, Inc. 1973-
ISSN: 0315-8888
FREQUENCY: 5 per yr.
ADDRESS: 284-810 W. Broadway, Vancouver, BC V5Z 4C9, Canada
TEL.: 604-925-0266   FAX: 604-925-0566
E-mail: rockland@mindlink.bc.ca

54

Gakkou Toshokan Sokuhoban (Japon / Japan)
Zenkoku Gakkou Toshokan Kyougikai (Japan School Library Association). Tokyo-to: Zenkoku Gakkou Toshokan Kyougikai, monthly. 1954-
ISSN: 0435-0405
FREQUENCY: monthly

Ganztagsschule (Allemagne / Germany)
Kassel: Ganztagsschulverband Gemeinnuetzige Gesellschaft Tagesheimschule e. V., 1961-
ISSN: 0344-2101
FREQUENCY: Quarterly
ADDRESS: Quellhofstr. 140, 34127 Kassel, Germany
TEL.: 0561-85077

IFLA Section of School Libraries. Newsletter (International)
International Federation of Library Associations and Institutions - Section of School Libraries, 1977-
ADDRESS: c/o Professor Blanche Woolls, Editor
School of Libray and Information Studies, University of Pittsburgh, 135 N. Bellefield Avenue, Pittsburgh, PA 15260 USA
FREQUENCY: 2 per yr.
TEL.: FAX:

Impact (Canada)
Vancouver: Association for Teacher-Librarianship in Canada, 1990-
ISSN: 1191-8063
FREQUENCY: Quarterly
ADDRESS: 782 Warwick St., Woodstock ON N4S 4R1
TEL.: 519-421-2219 FAX: 519-539-7226

Inter BCD Revue des bibliothèques centres documentaires (France)
Étampes: CEDIS, 1995-
ISSN: 1270-1467
FREQUENCY: Quaterly
ADDRESS: 2, résidence de Guinette, 91150 Estampes, France
TEL.: 33- 1-64-94-39-51 FAX: 33-1-64-94-49-35

Inter CDI. Revue des centres de documentation et d'information scolaires (France)
Étampes: CEDIS, 1972-
ISSN: 0242-2999
FREQUENCY: bi-m.
ADDRESS: 2, résidence de Guinette, 91150 Estampes, France
TEL.: 33-1-64-94-39-51
FAX: 33-1-64-96-49-35
Formerly (until 1974): Inter SDI (ISSN: 1154-7758).

Journal of Educational Media and Library Sciences = Jiaoyu Ziliao yu Tushuguan Xue
(République populaire de Chine / Republic of China)
Tamsui, Taipei, Taiwan: Tamkang University; Graduate Institute of Educational Media and Library Sciences; Chueh Sheng Memorial Library, 1970-
ISSN: 1013-090X
FREQUENCY: Quarterly
ADDRESS: 25137, Republic of China FAX: 02-622-6149
Text in Chinese and English; summaries in English
Formerly (until 1982): Journal of Educational Media Sciences: ISSN 0377-9890

Letters for the School Librarians (Israel)
[In Hebrew]
Jerusalem,
ISSN: 0792-6537

Library Talk: the magazine for elementary school libraries (États-Unis / United States)
Worthing, OH: Linworth Publishing, 1988-
ISSN: 1043-237X
FREQUENCY: Bimonthly
ADDRESS: 480 E. Wilson Bridge Rd., Ste L., Worthington, OH 43085
TEL.: 614-436-7107; 800-768-5017   FAX: 614-436-9490

Lire au collège   (France)
Grenoble: Centre Régional de Documentation Pédagogique
ISSN: 0754-1384
FREQUENCY: Irregular

Lire au lycée   (France)
Grenoble: Centre Régional de Documentaion Pédagogique
ISSN: 0762-9532
FREQUENCY: Irregular

Lire au lycée professionnel   (France)
Grenoble: Centre Régional de Documentation Pédagogique
ISSN: 1145-0428
FREQUENCY: Irregular

Majalah IPI. School Library Division   (Indonésie / Indonesia)
Jakarta: Ikatan Pustakawan Indonesia.
ISSN: 0126-1207
FREQUENCY: Semi-annual

Médiadoc   (France)
Paris: Fédération des Enseignants Documentalistes de l'Éducation nationale (FADBEN), 1989-
ISSN: 1260-7649
FREQUENCY: 2 per yr.
ADDRESS: FADBEN, B.P. 129   75 223 Paris Cédex 05 France
Publ.: *Médiadoc*
TEL. et FAX : 33-1-43 72 45 60

Media Focus = Mediafokus   (Afrique du Sud / South Africa)
Pretoria: South African School Media Association, 1969-
Text in Afrikaans, English
ISSN: 1016-8206
FREQUENCY: Semiannual
ADDRESS: c/o Education Media Service, Private Bag X290, Pretoria 0001, South Africa
FAX: 27-12-3227699
Former titles (until 1988): *School Media Centre* (until 1980); *School Library*   ISSN 0036-6617

Newsletter of the School Libraries Group   (Trinidad et Tobago / Trinidad and Tobago)
Library Association of Trinidad and Tobago - School Libraries Group
ADDRESS: P.O. Box 1275, Port of Spain, Trinidd and Tobago
FREQUENCY: monthly.   Source: *Connections*

Nieuwsbrief   (Pays Bas / Netherlands)
Landelijke Werkgroep Schoolbibliothecarissen voortgezet onderwijs Lindelaan la.
FREQUENCY: 3 per yr.   Source: *Connections*

Nigerian School Library Journal   (Nigeria)
Ibadan: Nigerian School Library Asociation, 1977-
ISSN: 0331-8214
FREQUENCY: Semiannual

Orana: Australia's national journal of school and children's librarianship   (Australie / Australia)
Queen Victoria Terrace: Australian Library and Information Association, 1965-
ISSN: 0045-6705
FREQUENCY: Quarterly
ADDRESS: P.O. Box E 441, Queen Victoria Terrace, A.C.T. 2600, Australia
TEL.: (07) 3201 8420   (International + 61 7 3201 4492)
FAX: (07) 3201 4492
http://www.alia.org.au/publications/orana/home.html or http://babs.com.au/orana
Formerly: *Children's Libraries Newsletter*   ISSN 0045-6705

Le Parola e il Libro (The Word and the Book)   (Italie / Italy)
Ente Nazionale per la Biblioteche Poplari e Scolastiche (National Group for Public and School
Libraries).   Source: *Connections*

Presidential Hotline   (États-Unis / United States)
American Association of School Librarians, American Library Association
50 East Huron Street Chicago IL 60611-2795   USA
TEL.: 800-545-2433, ext: 4381   312-280-4381   FAX: 312-664-7459

Sahifat al-Maktabat (EgyptianLibrary Journal)   (Égypte / Egypt)
Cairo: Egyptian School Library Association. (Text in Arabic; Summaries in English). 1969-
ISSN: 0531-6723
FREQUENCY: Quaterly.
ADDRESS: 35 al-Galaa St., Cairo, Egypt
TEL.: 753 001

SCAN: Curriculum Resources and Information Services   (Australie / /Australia)
NSW Department of School Education, 1952-
!SSN: 0726-4127
FREQUENCY: 4 per yr.

School Librarian   (Royaume Uni / United Kingdom)
Swindon: School Library Association, 1937-
ISSN: 0036-6595
FREQUENCY: 4 per yr.
ADDRESS: The School Library Association, Liden Library, Barrington Close, Liden,
Swindon SN3 6HF, England.
TEL.: 01793-617838
Formerly: School Librarian and School Library Review.

School Librarian's Workshop   (États-Unis / United States)
Berkeley Heights, NJ: Library Learning Resources, 1980-
ISSN: 0271-3667
FREQUENCY: m. (except Jul.-Aug.)
ADDRESS: Library Learning Resources, Inc., 61 Greenbriar Dr., Box 87, Berkeley Heights, NJ 07922
TEL.: 201-635-1833   FAX: 201-635-2614

School Libraries in Canada   (Canada)
Ottawa: Canadian School Library Association, vol. 17, 1974-
ISSN: 0227-3780
FREQUENCY: Quarterly
ADDRESS: 200 Elgin St., Ottawa, Ontario, K2P 1L5 Canada
TEL.: 613-232-9625   FAX: 603-563-9895
Formerly (until 1980): *Moccasin Telegraph*   ISSN 0076-9878

School Libraries in view (Royaume Uni / United Kingdom)
London: Library Association, School Libraries Group 1980 -
ISSN: 0261 -1687
FREQUENCY: Semiannual
ADDRESS: 148 Annandale Road, London SE10 OJZ, England.
Formerly : *School Libraries Group News* ISSN 0261-1678

School libraries worldwide (International)
International Association of School Librarianship
ISSN: 1023-9391
FREQUENCY: 2 per yr.
ADDRESS: International Association of School Librarianship, Suite 300   P.O. Box 34069
Seattle, Washington 98124-1069 USA
URL: http://www.rhi.hi.is/~anne/linksiasl.html
TEL.: (604) 925 0266   FAX: (604) 925 0566   E-mail: iasl@rockland.com

School Library Association Newsletter (Papouasie Nouvelle Guinée / Papua New Guinea)
J.A. Evans, SPCenCIID, P.O. Box 320, University PO
                    Source: *Connections + IASL Directory 1996*

***School Library Journal: the magazine of children, young adults & school librarians = S L J,
School Library Journal*** (États-Unis / United States)
New York, NY: Cahners Publishing Company, 1954-
ISSN: 0362-8930
FREQUENCY: 12 per yr.
ADDRESS: Box 57559, Boulder, CO 80322-7559
TEL.: 800-456-9409; 212-645-0067   FAX: 212-242-7216
E-mail: schlibj@class.org

School Library Media Activities Monthly (États-Unis / United States)
Baltimore, MD: LMS Associates, 1984-
ISSN: 0889-9371
FREQUENCY: m. (10 per yr.)
ADDRESS: 17 E. Henrietta St., Baltimore, MD 21230
TEL.: 410-685-8621

School library media annual (États-Unis / United States)
Englewood, CO: Libraries Unlimited, Inc., 1982-
ISSN: 0739-7712
FREQUENCY: Annual
ADDRESS: Box 6633, Englewood, CO 80155-6633
TEL.: 800-237-6124   FAX: 303-220-8843

School Library Media Quarterly (États-Unis / United States)
American Association of School Librarians, American Library Association. Chicago, IL: ALA, 1952-
ISSN: 0278-4823
FREQUENCY: 4 per yr.
ADDRESS: 50 E. Huron St., Chicago, IL 60611-2795
TEL.: 800-545-2433 FAX: 312-440-9374
Former titles: *School Media Quarterly* ISSN 0361-1647; *School Libraries*   ISSN 0036-6609

Schoolmediatheek (Pays Bas / Netherlands)
The Hague: Nederlands Bibliotheek en Lektuur Centrum, 1977-
ISSN: 0165-1099
FREQUENCY: 3 per yr.

Schulbibliothek Aktuell   (Allemagne / Germany)
Berlin: Deutsches Bibliotheksinstitut, Beratungsstelle für Schulbibliotheken (Department for School Libraries), 1975-
ISSN: 0341-471X
FREQUENCY: Quarterly
ADDRESS: Abt. 1-Publikationen, Alt-Moabit 101A, 10559 Berlin, Germany.
TEL.: 030-39077-0   FAX: 030-39077100

Skolebiblioteket (The School Library)   (Danemark / Denmark)
Bjert: Danmarks Skolebibliotekarforening (Association of Danish School Librarians), 1972-
ISSN: 0105-9556
FREQUENCY: 9 per yr.
ADDRESS: Mariajev 1, Sdr. Bjert, DK-6091 Bjert, Denmark
TEL.: 75-57-71-01

Skolebiblioteksåarbog (School Library annual)   (Danemark / Denmark)
Copenhagen: Danmarks Skolebiblioteksforening (Danish School Library Association) 1969-
ISSN: 0900-9582
FREQUENCY: Annual
ADDRESS: Vesterbrogade 20, DK 1620, Copenhagen V   Denmark
TEL.: 45-33 25 32 22   FAX: 45-33 25 32 23

Technology Connection: the newsletter for school library media specialists   (États-Unis / United States)
Worthington, OH: Linworth Publishing, 1994-
ISSN: 1074-4851
FREQUENCY: m. (exc. July & Aug.)
ADDRESS: 480 E. Wilson Bridge Rd., Ste L. Worthington, OH 43085

Uganda School Library Association Newsletter   (Ouganda / Uganda)
Uganda School Library Association
FREQUENCY: 4 per yr.
ADDRESS: c/o Public Libraries Board, Bugunda Road, P.O. Box 4262
Kampala, Uganda

3.2

REVUES EN BIBLIOTHÉCONOMIE SCOLAIRE
Index des pays

PERIODICALS IN SCHOOL LIBRARIANSHIP
Index of Countries

Avec la collaboration de : With the collaboration of :

Niels Jacobsen, Benoit Létourneau, Richard Morin, Robert Roy et Guylaine Vinet

---

International	- *IFLA Section of School Libraries. Newsletter.* - *School libraries worldwide.*
Afrique du Sud / South Africa	- *Media Focus = Mediafokus*
Allemagne / Germany	- *Ganztagsschule* - *Schulbibliothek Aktuell*
Australie / Australia	- *Access. Australian School Library Association* - *Orana: Australia's national journal of school and children's librarianship* - *SCAN: Curriculum Resources and Information Services*
Bermudes / Bermuda	- *Bermuda Association of School Librarians.*
Canada	- *Bookmark* - *Emergency librarian* - *Impact* - *School Libraries in Canada*
Chili / Chile	- *ABIEP. Boletin*
Chine (République de) / China (Republic of)	- *Journal of Educational Media and Library Sciences = Jiaoyu Ziliao yu Tushuguan Xue*
Croatie / Croatia	- *Bulletin of School Librarians.*
Danemark / Denmark	- *Boern og Boeger (Children and Books)* - *Skolebiblioteket (The School Library)* - *Skolebiblioteksårbog (School Library Annual)*
Égypte / Egypt	- *Sahifat al-Maktabat (Library Journal)*
Espagne / Spain	- *Educacion y Biblioteca*
États-Unis / United States	- *Book Report: journal for junior and senior high school librarians* - *College and Undergraduate Libraries* - *Community and Junior College Libraries: the journal for learning resource centers* - *Library Talk: the magazine for elementary school libraries* - *Presidential Hotline* - *School Librarian's Workshop* - *School Library Journal: the magazine of children, young adults and school librarians*

États-Unis / United States (suite / continued)	- *School Library Media Activities Monthly* - *School library media annual* - *School Library Media Quarterly* - *Technology Connection: the newsletter for school library media specialists*
France	- *Les actes de lecture* - *Argos: revue des B C D et des C D I* - *Choisir* - *Inter BCD. Revue des bibliothèques centres documentaires* - *Inter CDI. Revue des centres de documentation et d'information scolaires* - *Lire au collège* - *Lire au lycée* - *Lire au lycée professionnel* - *Médiadoc*
Indonésie / Indonesia	- *Majalah IPI*
Israel	- *Letters for the School Librarians*
Italie / Italy	- *Le Parola e il Libro (The Word and the Book)*
Japon / Japan	- *Gakkou Toshokan Sokuhoban*
Nigéria / Nigeria	- *Nigerian School Library Journal*
Ouganda / Uganda	- *UgandaSchool Library Association Newsletter*
Papouasie Nouvelle Guinée / Papua New Guinea	- *School Library Association. Newsletter*
Pays Bas / Netherlands	- *Nieuwsbrief* - *Schoolmediatheek*
Royaume Uni / United Kingdom	- *Education Libraries Journal* - *School Librarian* - *School Libraries in View*
Suède / Sweden	- *Barn och Kultur = Children and Culture*
Trinidad et Tobago Trinidad and Tobago	- *Newsletter of the School Libraries Group*

Quatrième partie / Part Four

~~~

Ressources sur les Bibliothèques et centres documentaires scolaires à travers le monde

~~~

Resources about School Libraries and Resource Centers around the World

~~~

Base de données créée et gérée par :   Database Created and Managed by :
Benoit Létourneau

Nous remercions les personnes suivantes
qui ont particulièrement contribué à cette partie :

We thank the following persons
who have greatly contributed to this part :

- **préparation des listes / work on the lists**
  Lucie David, Benoit Létourneau, Richard Morin,
  Alexandra Papazoglou, Marguerite Tremblay

- **création et gestion de la base de données -
  édition et index
  creating and managing the database -
  editing and indexes**
  Benoit Létourneau

- **correction et révision / correction and revision**
  Colette Charrier, Margarethe Dahlström, Lyn Hay,
  Teruyo Horikawa, Niels Jacobsen, Torny Kjekstad,
  Inci Önal, Glenys Willars

- **identification de nouveaux documents
  identifying new documents**
  Lin Forrest, Anne M. Galler, Ramon Salaberria

4.1
RESSOURCES SUR LES BIBLIOTHÈQUES ET CENTRES DOCUMENTAIRES SCOLAIRES À TRAVERS LE MONDE
International-régional et pays, répertoires et bibliographies

RESOURCES ABOUT SCHOOL LIBRARIES AND RESOURCE CENTERS AROUND THE WORLD
Intenational-Regional and Countries, Directories and Bibliographies

Base de données créée et gérée par :   Database Created and Managed by :

Benoit Létourneau

INTRODUCTION

Cette partie résulte du projet "Bibliothèques scolaires à travers le monde" dont l'objectif principal était de recenser les normes et lignes directrices, les politiques, les lois, décrets et règlements, les rapports et tout autre document de portée générale relatifs aux bibliothèques et centres documentaires scolaires parus depuis 1980 à travers le monde.

Ce projet a démarré à partir des références citées dans les communications du pré-séminaire de Caldes de Montbui tenu en août 1993, auxquelles ont été intégrées celles fournies par les membres du bureau de la Section des bibliothèques scolaires, ainsi que celles provenant de l'enquête sur les politiques en matière de bibliothèques scolaires menée par Anne Galler en 1994 pour le compte de la Bibliothèque nationale du Canada. Les références ainsi collectées ont été versée dans une base de données créée et gérée par Benoit Létourneau à l'aide du logiciel Pro-Cite, version 2.0. La version imprimée de la base a été soumise à trois révisions par les membres du bureau de la Section et par des personnes-ressources en août 1995, février 1996 et août 1996. Nous les remercions chaleureusement de leur collaboration.

La version que vous avez entre les mains date de juin 1997 et contient 455 notices bibliographiques qui se répartissent comme suit: 65 à caractère multinational et international, 383 provenant de 63 pays et 7 répertoires ou bibliographies (pour plus de détail, voir le tableau de la page suivante).

Comme de nombreux documents en bibliothéconomie scolaire sont des publications non commerciales, il n'a pas toujours été possible de retrouver les signalements complets de ceux que nous n'avions pas entre les mains. Nous avons cependant conservé certaines notices incomplètes en raison de leur intérêt. Pour que nous puissions continuer à tenir la base à jour et à en améliorer la qualité, nous vous serions reconnaissants de nous faire part des erreurs et omissions que vous constaterez, ainsi que des nouveaux titres dont vous aurez connaissance.

In the following pages, you will find the result of the "Project School Libraries in the World" which aimed at identifying standards and guidelines, policies, laws and decrees, reports of the state of school libraries and resource centers and other documents of general scope published since 1980 around the world.

The project begun with the citations from the papers given during the Pre-Session Seminar in Caldes de Montbui in August 1993, to which were added the references collected by the members of the Standing Committee of the Section of School Libraries and those received by Anne Galler during the survey of school library policies that she conducted on behalf of the National Library of Canada. All the references collected have been entered into a database created and managed by Benoit Létourneau with the Pro-Cite software, version 2.0. The printed output of the database has been revised three times by the members of the Section and by resource persons, in August 1995, February 1996 and August 1996. We thank them warmly for their collaboration.

The version you have in your hands is dated June, 1997 and contains 455 references distributed as follows: 65 of international or multinational interest, 383 from 63 countries, and 7 directories or bibliographies (for more detail, see the table on next page).

Considering that many documents in school librarianship are non commercial publications, it was not always possible to find the complete bibliographic description of those we did not have in hand. We have nonetheless kept some incomplete citations because of their interest. In order to help us keep the database up-to-date and to improve its quality, please notify us of any errors and omissions that you notice, and send us the references of new relevant titles you are aware of.

RÉPARTITON DES RÉFÉRENCES - DISTRIBUTION OF THE REFERENCES

		1 Pol. Edu.	2 Nor/Lign	3 L/D/R/	4 Situation	5 Rap./Rep.	Total
International/mulinational	International/multinational	1	10		15	39	65
Afrique du Sud	South Africa		1		1	1	3
Allemagne	Germany				1	2	3
Argentine	Argentina	2	1		1	3	7
Australie	Australia	1	11		4	13	29
Belgique	Belgium		1			2	3
Botswana	Botswana		2		3	1	6
Brésil	Brazil			1	1	4	6
Canada	Canada	4	35		6		45
Chili	Chile	2			2	1	5
Chine	China		1		3		4
Colombie	Colombia				1		1
Corée	Korea				1		1
Costa Rica	Costa Rica				1		1
Cuba	Cuba		2		2		4
Danemark	Denmark	1	1	3		3	8
El Salvador	El Salvador		1				1
Espagne	Spain	1	2	9	2		14
Estonie	Esthonia		1		1		2
États-Unis d'Amérique	United States of America		19	2	1	8	30
Ethiopie	Ethiopia				1		1
Finlande	Finland				1	1	2
France	France		6	1	5	27	39
Ghana	Ghana				1		1
Hongrie	Hungary		2		1	1	4
Iles Fidji	Fiji		1		1	1	3
Inde	India			1	1	1	3
Indonésie	Indonesia	1					1
Iran	Iran					1	1
Islande	Iceland				4		4
Israël	Israel		1	1	2		4
Italie	Italia	1	1				2
Jamaïque	Jamaica	3	1		2	3	9
Japon	Japan		2	2	1	4	9
Jordanie	Jordan				2		2
Kazakstan	Kazakstan	1					1
Kenya	Kenya				1		1
Liban	Lebanon				1		1
Malaisie	Malaysia	1			1	2	4
Mexique	Mexico		1			2	3
Myanmar	Myanmar				1		1
Namibie	Namibia		1		5		6
Nigéria	Nigeria	1	2		2	7	12
Norvège	Norway	5	4	6	1	4	20
Nouvelle Zélande	New Zealand				1	2	3
Papouasie-Nouvelle-Guinée	Papua New Guinea				1	2	3
Pérou	Peru				1	1	2
Portugal	Portugal		1	1		1	3
Quatar	Quatar		1				1
République d'Irlande	Republic of Ireland		1				1
Royaume -Uni	United Kingdom	7	15		6	8	36
Russie	Russia		2				2
Sénégal	Senegal				1	1	2
Sierra Leone	Sierra Leone				1		1
Singapour	Singapore		1				1
Suède	Sweden		2	1		3	6
Suisse	Switzerland		1		1		2
Swaziland	Swaziland				1	3	4
Thaïlande	Thailand		1				1
Trinidad et Tobago	Trinidad et Tobago	1	1				2
Tunisie	Tunisia				1		1
Turquie	Turquish				3		3
Venezuela	Venezuela				1		1
Zimbabwe	Zimbabwe				1		1
Répertoires/Bibliographies	Directories/Bibliographics					7	7
Total		33	137	28	104	153	455

Sources à caractère international ou multinational / International or multinational sources

1. *Politiques générales d'éducation / General Educational Policies*

   1. Organización de Estados Americanos. *Modelo flexible para un sistema nacional de bibliotecas escolares: Colombia, Costa Rica, Perú, Venezuela.* S.l: OEA, s.d., 318 p.

2. *Politiques, normes et lignes directrices en bibliothéconomie scolaire*
Policies, Standards and Guidelines in School Librarianship

   2. Bernhard, Paulette. *The section of School Libraries: goals, objectives and actions*, 5p. (paper given at the Open Forum of the Division serving the general public, 60th IFLA Conference, La Habana, Cuba, August 21-27, 1994).

   3. Carroll, Frances Laverne. *Guidelines for school libraries.* The Hague: International Federation of Library Associations and Institutions, 1990. 37 p. (IFLA professional reports; no. 20).
Note: Traduit en italien (1995) et en arabe (1996).

   4. Galler, Anne M. "National school library policies: an international survey." *IFLA Journal*, vol. 22, no. 4, 1996, pp. 292-298.

   5. Hannesdottir, Sigrun Klara. *Guidelines for the education and training of school librarians.* The Hague : IFLA, 1986. 47 p. (IFLA professional reports; no.9).
Note: Nouvelle édition révisée en 1995 / revised in 1995.

   6. ___. *School librarians : guidelines for competency requirements.* The Hague : IFLA, 1995. 46 p. (IFLA professional reports; no. 41).

   7. ___ (Ed.). *Guidelines for conducting national surveys of school libraries and their needs.* Paris : UNESCO, 1994, 115 p. (CII-94/WS/7).

   8. International Association of School Librarianship. *A policy statement on school libraries.* Originally accepted by IASL Board of Directors, August 1983. Revised IASL, September 1993. Kalamazoo, MI : IASL. 3 p.

   9. International Book Committee. *Recommendation on school libraries.* Genève : IBC, 1995. 2 p.

  10. International Federation of Library Associations and Institutions. Section of Children's Libraries. *Guidelines for library services for young adults.* The Hague : IFLA, [1996]. 11 p.

  11. "Resolutions of the IFLA Pre-session Seminar on School Librarianship : Issues for Developing Countries. Caldes de Montbui, Spain, 15-20 August, 1993". *IFLA express*, no. 4, Aug. 24, 1993, pp. 4-5.
Note: Traduction: Résolutions du Séminaire de pré-session de l'IFLA sur les bibliothèques scolaires. Caldes de Montbui (Espagne), 16-20 août 1993. 5 p.

4. *Situation des bibliothèques scolaires et des centres documentaires scolaires*
Situation of School Libraries and Resource Centers

  12. Abdel-Motey, Yaser. "Education for school librarianship : the core and competency-based education." *International review of children's literature and librarianship*, vol. 5, no. 1, 1990, pp. 1-11.

  13. Bernhard, Paulette. "Bibliothèques scolaires en action : quelques réalisations. 1. Angleterre et États-Unis." *Argus*, vol. 22, no. 3, Hiver 1993-94, pp. 13-18.

  14. ___. "Bibliothèques scolaires en action : quelques réalisations. 2e partie : France et Canada." *Argus*, vol. 23, no. 2, 1994, pp. 27-34.

Sources à caractère international ou multinational (suite)
International or multinational sources (continued)

4. *Situation des bibliothèques scolaires et des centres documentaires scolaires (suite)*
   Situation of School Libraries and Resource Centers (continued)

15. "Les CDI aux Pays-Bas et en Belgique." *Inter-CDI* , no. 115, janvier-février 1992, pp. 57-61.

16. Dike, Virginia W. *Issues in school librarianship in the developing countries*, 14 p. (paper given at the IFLA Pre-session seminar on School Librarianship : Issues for Developing Countries, Caldes de Montbui, Spain, August 15-20, 1993).

17. Faseh, Mary. *Issues in stocking school libraries*, 23 p. (paper given at the IFLA Pre-session seminar on School Librarianship : Issues for Developing Countries, Caldes de Montbui, Spain, August 15-20, 1993).

18. Fernandez de Zamora, Rosa María. "Library resources in Latin America : a general panorama." *IFLA journal* , vol. 17, no. 1, 1991, pp. 45-54.

19. Hannesdottir, Sigrun Klara. *Education for school librarians : a scandinavian perspective*, 18 p. (paper given at the17th annual Conference of the International Association of School Librarianship, Kuala Lumpur, Malaysia, July 22-26, 1989).

20. Horowitz, Rosario Gassol de. "The school library and NATIS in developing countries : the need for integration." *IFLA journal* , vol. 5, no. 1, 1979, pp. 22-29.

21. Isaza de Pedraza, Mary Luz. *El financiamiento de las bibliotecas escolares en países en desarrollo*. 34 p. (paper given at the IFLA Pre-session seminar on School Librarianship : Issues for Developing Countries, Caldes de Montbui, Spain, August 15-20, 1993).

22. Lowrie, Jean E. and Mieko Nagakura, (Ed.). *School libraries : international developments*. 2nd ed. Metuchen, N.J. : Scarecrow Press, Inc., 1991. 393 p.
    Note: Situation des bibliothèques scolaires dans les régions suivantes / situation of school libraries in the following regions:
    1) Europe: Allemagne fédérale / Federal Republic of Germany, Danemark / Denmark, Finlande / Finland, Islande / Iceland, Norvège / Norway, Royaume-Uni / United Kingdom, Suède / Sweden;
    2) Afrique / Africa: Afrique du Sud / Republic of South Africa, Nigéria / Nigeria, Tanzanie / Tanzania;
    3) Asie / Asie: Hong Kong, Inde / India, Israël / Israel, Japon / Japan, Jordanie / Jordan, Malaisie / Malaysia, République Populaire de Chine / People's Republic of China, Singapour / Singapore, Thaïlande / Thailand;
    4) Océanie / Oceania: Australie / Australia, Nouvelle-Zélande / New Zealand, Pacifique Sud / South Pacific Island Nations;
    5) Amérique du Nord / North America: Canada, États-Unis / United States.

23. Singh, Diljit. *The State of the world's school libraries*. International Association of School Librarianship, 21 p. (paper given at the 23rd annual Conference of the International Association of School Librarianship, Pittsburg, United States, July 17-22, 1994).

24. ___. *An international comparative study of school libraries*, Ph.D. Dissertation, Library studies, Florida State University, 1993.

25. Wright, J. "School librarianship : an international perspective." *School libraries in Canada* , vol. 9, no 2, 1989, pp. 25-30.

26. Zachary Pretlow, Delores. *Management Issues in School Librarianship*, 12 p. (paper given at the IFLA Pre-session seminar on School Librarianship : Issues for Developing Countries, Caldes de Montbui, Spain, August 15-20, 1993).

Sources à caractère international ou multinational (suite)
International or multinational sources (continued)

5. Rapports et autres documents / Reports and Other Documents

27. Adcock, Donald C. *School libraries and networking in North America: principles and problems of participation.* (paper given at the Open session of the Section of School Libraries, 48th IFLA General Conference, Montreal, 1982) (98/SCHO/ROTNAC/1-E).

28. Amey, J. Larry, (Ed.). *Combining libraries : the Canadian and Australian experience.* Halifax : Dalhousie University, School of library and information studies, Metuchen, N.J. : Scarecrow Press, 1987. 453 p. (Dalhousie University, SLIS series).

29. ___. *Quo vadis. South Australia's school community libraries : observations from a 1994 study tour.* Underdale: University of South Australia Library, 1994. 25 p.

30. Bernhard, Paulette. *Vers une nouvelle philosophie pédagogique: la bibliothèque/centre d'information en milieu scolaire,* In: Biennale de l'éducation et de la formation: débats sur les recherches et les innovations, Paris, UNESCO, 27-30 avril 1992. Résumés des communications. Paris : APRIEF, 1992, pp. 41-42.

31. ___. *La coopération entre les bibliothèques scolaires et bibliothèques publiques et un mot sur les bibliothèques combinées,* 5 p. (paper given at the Open Forum of the Division serving the general public, 60th IFLA Conference, La Habana, Cuba, August 21-27, 1994).

32. ___. "Mission, rôle et fonction de la bibliothèque/centre d'information (BCI) en milieu scolaire." In: *Colloque pour la mise en place d'une politique nationale des bibliothèques scolaires au Sénégal. Actes du colloque tenu au Cours Saint Marie de Hann les 6-7-8-9 avril 1994.,* Dakar (Sénégal): Ministère de l'Éducation nationale, 1994, pp. 41-43.

33. ___. "Vers une stratégie de formation. Deux clientèles cibles : les enseignants et les personnels des BCI." In: *Colloque pour la mise en place d'une politique nationale des bibliothèques scolaires au Sénégal. Actes du colloque tenu au Cours Saint Marie de Hann les 6-7-8-9 avril 1994,* Dakar (Sénégal): Ministère de l'Éducation nationale, 1994, pp. 48-49.

34. ___. "Bibliothèques, centres documentaires, centres d'information en milieu scolaire: aperçus internationaux." *Perspectives documentaires en sciences de l'éducation,* no. 31, 1994, pp. 90-109.

35. Bernhard, Paulette et Lise Breton (collab). *Le bibliothécaire/spécialiste de l'information en milieu scolaire : normes et lignes directrices, compétences, formation : contexte international, États-Unis, France, Royaune-Uni, Canada.* Montréal : Université de Montréal, École de bibliothéconomie et des sciences de l'information, 1991. 3 vol., 116 + 112 + 8 p.

36. ___. "The school media/information specialist : a comparison of standards and guidelines about personnel, competencies and education : international level, United States of America, France, United Kingdom, and English speaking provinces of Canada." *School library media annual,* vol. 12, 1994, pp. 244-272.

37. Clyde, Laurel A. (Ed.). *Sustaining the vision: a collection of articles and papers on research in school librarianship in honor of Jean E. Lowrie.* Castle Rock, CO : Hiwillow Research and Publishing, 1996. VI-332 p.

38. Dankert, Birgit. *Effective Management and Use of Secondary School Libraries.* Report of the Nairobi Workshop, held in the Goethe Institute, Nairobi, April - 10 May, 1985. (paper given at the Open session of the Section of School Libraries, 51st IFLA General Conference, Chicago, 1985) (180-SCHO-2-E).

39. Duces, Brigitte. "Word Bank activities in library and documentation services provision in developing countries." *Government information quarterly,* vol. 8, no. 4, 1991, pp. 381-386.

Sources à caractère international ou multinational (suite)
International or multinational sources (continued)

5. Rapports et autres documents (suite) / Reports and Other Documents (continued)

40. Education of school librarians : some alternatives. (papers presented at the seminar for the education of school librarians for Central America an Panama at San José, Costa Rica, 3-8 December 1978). München : Saur, 1982. 120 p. (IFLA publications; no 22).

41. Galler, Anne M. and Joan M. Coulter. *Managing school librairies.* The Hague: IFLA, 1990, 68 p. (IFLA Professional Report; 17).
Titre français: *La bibliothèque scolaire. Administration, organisation, services.* (IFLA Professional Report; 23).
Titre espagnol: La administracion de las bibliotecas escolares. (IFLA Professional Report; 29).

42. Gawith, Gwen. *School libraries: Bridges or barriers?* (paper given at the 52nd IFLA Conference, Tokyo, 1986). (055-SCHO-1-E).

43. Hall, Noelene. *Teachers, information and school libraries.* Paris : UNESCO, 1986. 110 p. (PGI-86/WS /17).
Note: Traduction: Les enseignants, l'information et les bibliothèques scolaires. 1986. 89 p.

44. ___. *Teachers, information and school libraries.* (paper given at the Open session of the Section of School Libraries, 51st IFLA General Conference, Chicago, 1985). (180-SCHO-1-E) .

45. Harris, C. G. S. *Training in the use of information and documentation in primary and secondary schools.* Paris : UNESCO, 1986. 76 p. + annexes. (PGI-86/WS/28).

46. Haycock, Ken. *What works : research about teaching and learning through the school's library resource center.* Seattle, WA; Vancouver, B.C. : Rockland Press, 1992. 230 p.

47. Irving, Ann. *Instructional materials for developing information concepts and information handling skills in school children: an international study.* Paris : UNESCO, 1981. 64 p. (PGI-81/WS/32).

48. Knuth, Rebecca. "School librarianship and macro-level policy issues : international perspectives." *IFLA journal* , vol. 21, no. 4, Dec. 1995, pp. 290-295.

49. ___. Convergence and global ethics: the International Association of School Librarianship and the worldwide promotion of school libraries. Doctoral dissertation, Indiana University, 1995.

50. Koga, Setsuko. *Academic Achievement and the School Library: an International Study.* (paper given at the Open session of the Section of School Libraries, 55th IFLA General Conference, Paris, 1989). (031-SCHOOl-3-E+F+S).

51. Lauster, Astrid. *Dual use libraries : report on a joint project of public and school libraries,* 1992. 8 p.
Note: Enquête menée pour le compte de la Section des bibliothèques scolaires de l'IFLA : réponses de 21 pays / Survey conducted on the behalf of the IFLA Section of School Libraries: reply from 21 countries.

52. "Libraries and media around the world." *Ohio media spectrum* , vol. 39, no 4, 1987.
Note: (No. spécial - thematic issue).

53. Mahar, Mary Helen. "The world bank and school library services." *School library journal* , vol. 30, no 7, 1984, pp. 113-117.

54. Mathews, Anne. *Excellence on a Budget: School Library Services with Limited Resources.* (paper given at the Open session of the Section of School Libraries, 53rd IFLA General Conference, Brighton, 1987). (027-SCHOOl-2-R).

Sources à caractère international ou multinational (suite)
International or multinational sources (continued)

5. *Rapports et autres documents (suite) / Reports and Other Documents (continued)*

55. Mwathi, P. G. and D. G. Ng'ang'a. *School libraries in Africa: an overview*. (paper given at the Open session of the Section of School Libraries, 50th IFLA General Conference, Nairobi, 1984).

56. Reumer, Dick. *The Centralized Automation of National Centres to Networking in School Libraries*. (paper given at the Open session of the Section of School Libraries, 48th IFLA Conference, Montreal, 1982). (129/SCHO/ROTNAC/2-E).

57. Stenberg, Christina. *Literacy and the School Library: Librarians and Teachers together against illiteracy*. (paper given at the Open session of the Section of School Libraries, 56th IFLA Conference, Stockholm, 1990). (48-SCHOOL-2-E).

58. Thomas, Lucille C. *Cultural Heritage through literature*. The Hague : IFLA, Section of School Libraries, 1993. 21 p.

59. ___. *Multiculturalism: challenges and opportunities for school librarians*. (paper given at the Open session of the Section of School Libraries, 54th IFLA Conference, Sydney, 1988). (6-SCHOOL-1-E).

60. Trask, Margaret (Ed.). *Projet pilote concernant le développement des bibliothèques scolaires dans la région du Pacifique Sud : programmes de formation : proposition de cours no 1: cours sur l'exploitation des ressources documentaires et des bibliothèques destiné aux enseignants du primaire et du secondaire*. Paris : UNESCO, 1983, 165 p. (PG1-83/WS/11).

61. ___ (Ed.). *South Pacific Region Pilot Project on School Library Development : training - programmes for teachers : course 1: for all teachers on the use of information resources and libraries by teachers; course 2: for teacher trainees who wish to take school librarianship as a major in their teacher training course*. Paris : UNESCO, 1984. 661 p. (PGI-84/WS/13).

62. Trudel, Raymonde. "La bibliothèque scolaire peut-elle faire la différence pour améliorer la réussite des élèves?" *Argus* , vol. 24 , no. 2, 1995, pp. 23-27.

63. Tsesarskaja, G. L. *Cultural Heritage Through Literature*. (paper given at the Open session of the Section of School Libraries, 49th IFLA General Conference, Munich, 1983). (68-SCHOOL-1-E).

64. Valin, A. *Pedagogie de la lecture en zone rurale (Pedagogy of reading in a rural area)*. (paper given at the Open session of the Section of School Libraries, 55th IFLA General Conference, Paris, 1989). (018-SCHOOL-2-F+E+S).

65. Woolls, Blanche. *Literacy and School Libraries*. (paper given at the Open session of the Section of School Libraries, 56th IFLA Conference, Stockholm, 1990). (47-SCHOOL-1-E).

Afrique du Sud / South Africa

2. *Politiques, normes et lignes directrices en bibliothéconomie scolaire*
   Policies, Standards and Guidelines in School Librarianship

66. South Africa. *Media centre services*. Cape Town : Education Library Service, 1993.

70

Afrique du Sud (suite) / South Africa (continued)

4. Situation des bibliothèques scolaires et des centres documentaires scolaires
Situation of School Libraries and Resource Centers

67. Pretoria. Transvaal Education Department. Education Media Service. *School Library Media Centres in a new dispensation for library and information services.* Report compiled by T.J. Swart. 1994.
Note: Enquête menée en 1994 par Galler (1996).

5. Rapports et autres documents / Reports and Other Documents

68. Bawa, Rookaya. *The role of the public library in supporting education in the natal Region.* (paper given at the 22nd annual Conference of the International Association of School Librarianship, Adelaide, South Australia, September 27-30, 1993).

Allemagne / Germany

4. Situation des bibliothèques scolaires et des centres documentaires scolaires
Situation of School Libraries and Resource Centers

69. Dankert, Birgit, and Andreas Mittrowann. *ÖffentlicheBibliothekund Schule - neue Formen der Partnerschaft. (Public Libraries and Schools - new forms of partnership).* Dokumentation zum Expertenhearing by Birgit Dankert and Andreas Mittrowann. Gütersloh : Verlag Bertelsmann Stiftung, 1995.
Note: Enquête menée en 1994 par Galler (1996).

5. Rapports et autres documents / Reports and Other Documents

70. Breithaupt, Renate. *Zentrale Dienstleistungen für Schulbibliotheken in der Bundesrepublik Deutschland am Beispiel des Schulbibliothekarischen Arbeitsstelle der Stadbucherei Frankfurt am Main. (Centralized School Library Services in the Federal Republic of Germany as performed at the School Library Services Centre of the Stadbucherei Frankfurt am Main).* (paper given at the Open session of the Section of School Libraries, 53rd IFLA General Conference, Brighton, 1987).

71. Papandieck, Andreas. *Schulbibliotheken und Schulmediotheken in der Bundesrepublik Deutschland (New environment of learning through school library media centers in the Federal Republic of Germany).* (paper given at the Open session of the Section of School Libraries, 49th IFLA General Conference, Munich, 1983). (106-CHIL-5/SCHO-3/AVM-4-G).

Argentine / Argentina

1. Politiques générales d'éducation / General Educational Policies

72. Argentina. *Estatuto del docente: Ley No 14.473 y normas reglamentarias.* Buenos Aires: Sainte Claire, 1988.

73. Argentina. Buenos Aires (Provincia). Dirección General de Escuelas y Cultura. *Ley no 9319 y Decreto Reglamentario No 2446.* Dirección General de Escuelas y Cultura, 1979.

2. Politiques, normes et lignes directrices en bibliothéconomie scolaire
Policies, Standards and Guidelines in School Librarianship

74. Argentina. Dirección Nacional de Investigación. Experimentación y Perfeccionamiento Educativo. *La Biblioteca escolar: su misión actual y su organización.* Por Stella Maris Fernandez. Buenos Aires: Experimentación y Perfeccionamiento Educativo, 1980. 62 p. (Nuera Serie Estudios y documentos; 3).

Argentine (suite) / Argentina (continued)

4. *Situation des bibliothèques scolaires et des centres documentaires scolaires*
   Situation of School Libraries and Resource Centers

   75. Córdoba, Carlos A. "La biblioteca escolar en Argentina informe de situación". 4 p. (paper given at the IFLA Pre-session seminar on School Librarianship : Issues for Developing Countries, Caldes de Montbui, Spain, August 15-20, 1993).

5. *Rapports et autres documents / Reports and Other Documents*

   76. Argentina. Tierra del Fuego: Dirección de Bibliotecas Escolares. *Programa permanente de capacitación en bibliotecología.* Ushuaia, Argentina : Dirección de Bibliotecas Escolares, 1990. (8 módulos).

   77. "Biblioteca escolar: un centro de aprendizaje." *Boletín de la Comisión para el desarrollo de las bibliotecas escolares nacionales* , vol. 1, no 2/5, 1985, 44 p.
   Note: (número especial).

   78. Gazpio, Dora Estela, and Maria Eugenia Lamas. *Lista de encabezamientos de materia para bibliotecas escolares y públicas de Tierra del Fuego.* Ushuaia, Argentina : Consejo Territorial de Educación, 1990. non paginé. (Version préliminaire).

~~~~~~

Australie / Australia

1. *Politiques générales d'éducation / General Educational Policies*

   79. Australian Education Council. *Putting general education to work.* Carlton, Vic. : The Council, 1992.

2. *Politiques, normes et lignes directrices en bibliothéconomie scolaire*
   Policies, Standards and Guidelines in School Librarianship

   80. Australian Library and Information Association. School Libraries Section. *Information technology in schools : implications for teacher librarians.* Perth, Australia: ALIA, 1992. 92 p.

   81. Australian School Library Association. Australian Library and Information Association and Curriculum Corporation. *Learning for the future: developing information services in Australian schools.* Carlton, Vic. : Curriculum Corporation 1993. VI-58 p.

   82. Benneto, Liz and Mary Manning. *Learning for the future: teacher resource book.* Melbourne, Vic.: Australian Library Association, 1995.

   83. Kirk, Joyce, Barbara Poston-Anderson and Hilary Yerbury. *Into the 21st century : library and information services in schools.* Perth, Australia : Australian Library and Information Association, 1990. VI-88 p.

   84. New South Wales. Department of School Education. *Information skills through the library telecourse* (Kit). The Department, 1989.
   Note: Contient / includes : Workshop leader's manual; Information skills in the schools.
   31 p.; video, 54 minutes.

   85. Queensland. Department of Education. *Resource management for schools with teacher–librarians.* 6th ed. Brisbane, Queensland : The Department, 1991.

   86. ___. *Resource management for schools without teacher–librarians.* 6th ed. Brisbane, Queensland : The Department, 1992.

Australie (suite) / Australia (continued)

2. *Politiques, normes et lignes directrices en bibliothéconomie scolaire (suite)*
Policies, Standards and Guidelines in School Librarianship (continued)

87. ___. *Resources in learning. A focus on school development* Dir. by Brian Bahnisch. Ed. by Esme Amundsen. Brisbane, Queensland : The Department, 1992, 52 p.

88. Queensland. Department of Education. Curriculum Resource Services. *Resource management for secondary schools.* 5th ed. Brisbane, Queensland : The Department, 1990.

89. South Australia. Department of Education. *Toward resource—based learning.* Ed. by Jill Duffield and al. Millswood, S. Aust. : The Department, 1991, 26 p.

90. South Australia. Education Department. *Educating for the 21st century: a charter for public schooling in South Australia.* Adelaide, S. Aust. : The Department, 1991.

4. *Situation des bibliothèques scolaires et des centres documentaires scolaires*
Situation of School Libraries and Resource Centers

91. Australian School Library Association. Australian Library and Information Association and Curriculum Corporation. *A select survey of school library resource centres in Australia.* Millswood, S. Aust. : The Orphanage Teachers Centre, 1992. 80 p.

92. Dillon, Ken (Ed.). *School library automation in Australia: issues and results of the national surveys.* 2nd ed. Wagga Wagga : Centre for Information Studies, 1997. 250 p.

93. Kemeny, Linley. "Western Australian school library funding survey." *Australian library review* , vol. 9, no. 3, August 1992, pp. 209-217.

94. Nicholson, Fay. *An overview of the current situation in school libraries* [Australia], 20 p. (paper given at the IFLA Pre-session seminar on School Librarianship : Issues for Developing Countries, Caldes de Montbui, Spain, August 15-20, 1993).

5. *Rapports et autres documents / Reports and Other Documents*

95. Cane, Georgina. *The Australian Schools Catalogue Information Service (ASCIS): its environment, clients and services.* (paper given at the Open session of the Section of School Libraries, 54th IFLA Conference, Sydney, 1988). (60-SCHOOL-3-E).

96. *Cooperative planning and teaching.* Toowong, Queensland : SLAQ. July 1987. Videogramme, 120 minutes.

97. *Cooperative planning and teaching within the changing administration of Queensland Schools .* Toowong, Queensland: SLAQ. June 1989. Videogramme, 90 minutes.

98. Hallein, Joe and Judy Phillips. *The education and role of teacher librarians : an Australian perspective.* (paper given at the 18th annual Conference of the International Association of School Librarianship, Malaysia, July 22-26, 1989).

99. Hay, Lyn and James Henri. *Leadership for collaboration: making vision work.* (paper given at the Open session of the Section of School Libraries, 61st IFLA General Conference, Istanbul, August 20-26 1995).

100. Hay, Lyn and Henri James (Ed.). *A meeting of the minds : ITEC virtual conference '96 proceedings.* Belconnen, A.C.T. : Australian School Library Association, 1996, 232 p.

101. Henri, James. "Education for school librarianship in Australia : a viewpoint." *School libraries in Canada* , vol. 6, no. 2, 1986, pp. 20-24.

Australie (suite) / Australia (continued)

5. *Rapports et autres documents (suite) / Reports and Other Documents (continued)*

102. ___. *The teacher librarian as manager: a selection of case studies.* Wagga Wagga, NSW : Charles Sturt University, Centre for Information Studies, 1990.

103. ___. *Cooperative planning and teaching: Australian theory and practice.* Wagga Wagga, NSW : Charles Sturt University, Centre for Information Studies, 1990.

104. ___. *The school curriculum: a collaborative approach to learning.* 2nd ed. Wagga Wagga, NSW : Charles Sturt University, Centre for Library Studies, 1988. 140 p.

105. Henri, James (Ed.). *Collaborative teaching and learning : Australian secondary schools theory and practice,* Wagga Wagga, NSW : Charles Sturt University, Centre for Information Studies, 1992. 126 p. (Occasional Monograph; 12).

106. *Partnerships in the learning environment : some keys players.* Toowong, Queensland : SLAQ. October 1993. Videogramme, 90 minutes.

107. Todd, Ross J. "Information literacy and learning : IASL report of Australian research." *Impact*, no. 12, May 1995, pp. 23-27.

Belgique / Belgium

2. *Politiques, normes et lignes directrices en bibliothéconomie scolaire*
   Policies, Standards and Guidelines in School Librarianship

108. Bodart, Jacques et al. *Bibliothèque, Centre de documentation et d'information: guide pour une action de qualité.* Liège : Fédération de l'enseignement fondamental catholique, Secrétariat général de l'enseignement catholique, 1995. 21 p.

5. *Rapports et autres documents / Reports and Other Documents*

109. Association belge de Documentation. Groupe "Formation des Utilisateurs" et ReCoDA (Éd.). *La bibliothèque au coeur du projet pédagogique,* Compte rendu du colloque organise le 15 octobre 1996. Bruxelles. Gembloux: ABD, 1997. 43 p. + annexes.

110. Parent, Yvette. "Bibliothèques publiques et bibliothèques scolaires en Communauté française de Belgique." In: *Actes du Séminaire international sur la création de modèles de jumelages institutionnels à l'intention des bibliothèques du Susdet du Nord, Ottawa, 20-21 juin 1991.,* Ottawa : Banque internationale d'information sur les états francophones, 1991, pp. 41-46.

Botswana

2. *Politiques, normes et lignes directrices en bibliothéconomie scolaire*
   Policies, Standards and Guidelines in School Librarianship

111. Botswana. *The Revised National Policy on Education.* Gaborone : Government Printer, 1993. 49 p.

112. Motlhabane, Ratanang E. *Organising School Libraries : A Manual for Community Junior Secondary Schools.* Gaborone : Botswana National Library Services, 1991, 59 p.

74

Botswana (suite / continued)

4. *Situation des bibliothèques scolaires et des centres documentaires scolaires*
Situation of School Libraries and Resource Centers

113. Baffour-Awuah, Margaret. *The Book Box Service : Attempting to serve Primary School Library Needs*. [Gaborone : Government Printer, 1992]. 5 p.

114. Metzger, A. J. B. "The development of school libraries in Botswana." *School library conference proceedings*. Pietermaritzburg, South Africa : University of Natal, 1992, pp. 36-51.

115. ___. "The training of Teacher-Librarians for Community Junior Secondary Schools in Botswana." *African journal of library, archives and information science* , vol. 2, no. 2, pp. 141-147.

5. *Rapports et autres documents / Reports and Other Documents*

116. Baffour-Awuah, Margaret. "Proceedings of the Educational Libraries seminar held at Gaborone Sun, 29-30 April 1996. Gaborone : 1996.

~~~~~~

Brésil / Brazil

3. *Lois, décrets et règlements en matière de bibliothèques et de centres documentaires scolaires*
Laws, Decrees and Rules about School Libraries and Resource Centers

117. Brasil. São Paulo. Secretaria municipal de Educado. Dept de orientação técnica do ensino de 10 E 20 graus. *Legislação de ensino de 10 e 20 graus: atualizaçao*. São Paulo, Brazil : SE/CENP1984. v. 18.

4. *Situation des bibliothèques scolaires et des centres documentaires scolaires*
Situation of School Libraries and Resource Centers

118. Fragoso, Graça Maria. *Bibliothèque scolaire où êtes-vous?*. 14 p. (paper given at the IFLA Pre-session seminar on School Librarianship : Issues for Developing Countries, Caldes de Montbui, Spain, August 15-20, 1993).

5. *Rapports et autres documents / Reports and Other Documents*

119. Castro, Yeda. "A biblioteca escolar no contexto educational brasileiro." In: *Seminário nacional sobre bibliotecas escolares, 1, Brasil out, 1982*, pp. 49-70. Brasilia: Fundação Nacional Pró-Memória/Instituto Nacional do Livro, 1982.

120. Garcia, Edson Gabriel. *Biblioteca escolar, estrutura e funcionamento*. São Paulo : Loyola, 1993. 108 p.

121. Mariconi, M. L. "Instituicionalização da biblioteca escolar." In: *Seminário nacional sobre bibliotecas escolares, 1, Brasilia, out, 1982*. Brasilia: Fundação Nacional Pró-Memória/INC. 1982. pp. 49-70.

122. *Seminário nacional sobre bibliothecas escolares 1, Brasilia, 1982*. Brasilia : Instituto Nacional do Livro, 1982.

~~~~~~

Canada

1. *Politiques générales d'éducation / General Educational Policies*

Colombie-Britannique / British Columbia

123. British Columbia. Ministry of Education. *Year 2000: a framework for learning.* Vancouver, B.C. : The Ministry, 1990. 29 p.

Nouveau-Brunswick

124. Nouveau Brunswick. Ministère de l'Education. *L'école secondaire au Nouveau-Brunswick.* Frederictown, N.B. : Le Ministère, 1986.

Ontario

125. Ontario. Ministry of Education. *New horizons.* [Toronto, Ont. : The Ministry, 1995].

126. Ontario. Ministry of Education and training. *The common curriculum policies and outcomes, grades 1-9.* Toronto, Ont. : The Ministry, 1995. 112 p.

2. *Politiques, normes et lignes directrices en bibliothéconomie scolaire*
Policies, Standards and Guidelines in School Librarianship

127. Association for Teacher-Librarianship in Canada. *Students' bill of information rights.* [Vancouver, B.C. : ATLC, 1995]. 1p.
Note: Traduction française par Paulette Bernhard : *Les droits de l'élève à l'ère de l'information.* 1 p.

128. Canadian School Library Association. "Guidelines for effective school library programs. Rationale." *School libraries in Canada*, vol. 8, no 4, Summer 1988, p. 30.

129. ___. "Guidelines for effective school library programs. A glossary of terms." *School libraries in Canada*, vol. 9, no 3, Spring 1989, p. 45.

130. ___. *Guidelines for effective school library programs.* Ottawa : CSLA, 1994.

131. Doiron, Ray. "School library policies in Canada : a shared vision from sea to sea." *School libraries in Canada*, vol. 14, no. 1, Winter 1994, pp. 15-19.

132. "The qualifications for library technicians working in school systems : a policy statement approved by CSLA executive council and CLA Council, June 1984." *School libraries in Canada*, vol. 4, no. 4 (1984): pp. 13-16.

Alberta

133. Alberta Education. *Focus on learning: an integrated program model for Alberta school libraries.* Edmonton, Alta. : Alberta Education, Media and Technology branch, 1985. 67 p.

134. ___. *Policies, guidelines, procedures and standards for school libraries.* Edmonton, Alta : Alberta Education, 1984. 8 p.

Colombie-Britannique / British Columbia

135. British Columbia. Ministry of Education. Learning Resources Branch. *Developing independent learners.* Victoria, B.C. : The Ministry, 1991. 101 p.

Canada (suite / continued)

2. *Politiques, normes et lignes directrices en bibliothéconomie scolaire (suite)*
Policies, Standards and Guidelines in School Librarianship (continued)

136. British Columbia. Ministry of Education. Learning Resource Branch and British Columbia Teacher–Librarians' Association. *Resource–based learning and teaching.* Prince George, B.C. : BCTLA, 1994. 11 p.

137. Driscoll, Dianne (Ed.). *Implementing change : a cooperative approach to initiating, implementing and sustaining library resource centre programs.* Vancouver, B.C. : British Columbia Teacher-Librarians' Association, 1989. 170 p.

<u>Ile du Prince Edouard / Prince Edward Island</u>

138. Prince Edward Island. Department of Education. *School library policy for the province of Prince Edward Island.* Charlottetown. P.E.I. : The Department, 1989.

139. Prince Edward Island School Library Association; Teacher–Librarians for Regional School Units 1 to 4. *Toward the year 2000 : the role of the school–library resource–centre.* Charlottetown, P.E.I. : The Department, 1991. 24 p.

<u>Manitoba</u>

140. Manitoba Education and Training. Instructional Resources. *School library policy statement.* Winnipeg, Man. : The Ministry, 1991. 8 p.

141. Manitoba Education and Training. Instructional Resources Branch. *Guidelines for multicultural school library services.* Winnipeg, Man. : The Ministry, 1992. 24 p.
Note: Aussi disponible en français / Also available in French.

142. ___. *Resource–based learning : an educational model.* Winnipeg, Man. : The Ministry, 1994. 66 p.
Note: version en français:
Manitoba. Éducation et formation professionnelle. Direction des ressources éducatives. *L'apprentissage fondé sur les ressources: un modèle d'enseignement.* Winnipeg, Manitoba : Le Ministère, 1994. vi-63 p.

<u>Nouveau-Brunswick / New Brunswick</u>

143. Library Council of New Brunswick Teachers' Association. *Standards and practices for New Brunswick school libraries.* Fredericton, N.B.: The Library Council, 1991.

<u>Nouvelle-Écosse / Nova Scotia</u>

144. Nova Scotia School Library Association; Nova Scotia Teachers Union. *Nova Scotia school libraries: standards and practices.* Armdale, N.S. : NSSLA/NSTA, 1987. 24 p.

<u>Ontario</u>

145. Council of Ontario School Library Consultants. *Collaboration through partners in action: superintendent's guide.* Etobicoke, Ont. : Board of Education, 1992. 10 p.

146. ___. *Partners in Action: the second wave.* Aurora, Ont. : York Region Board of Education, 1991. 24 p.
Note: A position paper on *Partners in action: the library resource centre in the school curriculum.*

Canada (suite / continued)

**2. *Politiques, normes et lignes directrices en bibliothéconomie scolaire (suite)*
*Policies, Standards and Guidelines in School Librarianship (continued)***

147. Ontario. Ministry of Education. *Partners in action: the library resource centre in the school curriculum.* Toronto, Ont. : The Ministry, 1982. 52 p.
Note: version en français:
Ontario. Ministère de l'Éducation. *Intégration et coopération: le centre de ressources intégré à l'apprentissage.* Toronto, Ont. : Le Ministère, 1982. 48 p.

Québec / Quebec

148. Beaulac, Jacqueline, Paulette Bernhard, et Réal Gaudet. *La Bibliothèque scolaire: mission et objectifs : Document de réflexion.* Montréal : Association du personnel des services documentaires scolaires, 1991. 22 p.

149. Québec (Province). Comité d'étude sur les bibliothèques scolaires. *Les bibliothèques scolaires québécoises : plus que jamais. Rapport du comité d'étude.* Québec : Ministère de l'Éducation, Direction générale de l'évaluation des ressources didactiques, Direction des ressources didactiques, 1989. XXIV-216 p.

150. Québec (Province). Ministère de l'Éducation. Direction générale de l'évaluation et des ressources didactiques. Direction de la technologie éducative. *Les ressources documentaires : aspects pédagogiques et aspects organisationnels.* Par Yves Léveillé. Québec : Ministère de l'Éducation, 1987. 52 p. (Collection technologie éducative).
Note: version en anglais:
Québec. Ministère de l'Éducation. Direction générale de l'évaluation et des ressources didactiques. Direction de la technologie éducative. *Library resources in the schools: pedagogical and organizational aspects.* By Yves Léveillé. Québec : Le Ministère, 1987. 52 p. (Collection technologie éducative).

151. Québec (Province). Ministère de l'Éducation. Direction générale des ressources didactiques et de la formation à distance. *La bibliothèque de l'école : Un service de ressources et d'information.* Montréal : Le Ministère. 4 p.
Note: Version en anglais: School library : resources and information Services. 4 p.

Saskatchewan

152. Saskatchewan Association of Education Media Specialists. *The 4th R : resource–based learning : the library resource centre in the school curriculum.* Saskatoon, Sask. : Saskatchewan Teachers' Federation, 1986. 25 p.

153. Saskatchewan Education. *Resource-based learning. Policy, guidelines and responsibilities for Saskatchewan learning resource centres.* Regina, Sask. : Saskatchewan Education, [1987]. 18 p.

154. ___. *Learning resource centres in Saskatchewan : a guide for development.* Regina, Sask. : Saskatchewan Education, 1988. 88 p.

155. Saskatchewan Education. School Libraries Branch. Saskatchewan School Library Association. *Organizing for resource–based learning.* Regina, Sask. : Saskatchewan Education, 1991. 11 p.

156. Saskatchewan School Library Association. *School library and co–operative planning. Monograph No. 1.* Saskatoon, Sask. : SSLA, 1989. 20 p.

157. ___. *School library and co–operative planning. Monograph No. 2.* Saskatoon, Sask. : SSLA, 1989. 10 p.

Canada (suite / continued)

2. *Politiques, normes et lignes directrices en bibliothéconomie scolaire (suite)*
Policies, Standards and Guidelines in School Librarianship (continued)

158. ___. *Technology in the school library*. Dir. by Peter Reis. Saskatoon, Sask. : SSLA, 1990.
130 p.

Terre-Neuve et Labrador / Newfoundland and Labrador

159. Newfoundland and Labrador. Department of Education. Division of program development.
*Learning to learn. Policies and guidelines for the implementation of resource-based learning
in Newfoundland and Labrador schools.* St-John, Nfld. : The Department, 1991. IV-60 p.

160. Newfoundland and Labrador. Department of Education. Division of Program Development.
Learning to learn: implementation handbook. St. John's, Nfld. : The Department, 1992.
Note: Accompanied by VHS tape entitled *Resource bases learning, an overview*.

Territoires du Nord-Ouest / Northwest Territories

161. Northwest Territories. Ministry of Education. *Guidelines for the development of school library
information centres.* Yellowknife, N.W.T. : The Ministry. 9 p.

4. *Situation des bibliothèques scolaires et des centres documentaires scolaires*
Situation of School Libraries and Resource Centers

162. Haycock, Ken (Ed.). *Education of school librarianship in Canada*. Ottawa : Canadian Library
Association, 1983. 78 p.

163. Lightahll, Lynne. "Automated systems in Canada's school libraries : the fifth annual survey."
Feliciter, vol. 40, no. 11-12, Nov.-Dec. 1994, pp. 26-42.

164. Oberg, Dianne. "Education for teacher-librarians: a status report." *School libraries in Canada*,
vol. 9, no. 3, 1989, pp. 17-19.

165. Reade, Judith. "Finding out what it's really like : school library development in Nova Scotia,
1979-1981." *School libraries in Canada*, vol. 2, no. 2, 1982, pp. 18-20.

166. Ross, Leslie. "Manitoba school library services : a history." *School libraries in Canada*, vol. 2,
no. 3, 1982, pp. 10-11.

167. Wright, John C. "School libraries in Canada : an overview." *School libraries in Canada*, vol. 1,
no. 2, 1981, pp. 15-17.

Chili / Chile

1. *Politiques générales d'éducation / General Educational Policies*

168. Chile. Ministerio de Educacion. *Programa MECE. Orientaciones básicas, objetivos y
componentes. Documento de difusión.* Santiago: Ministerio de Educación, agosto 1991.
40 + 10 p.

169. Chile. Ministerio de Educación. *Educación de Calidad para todos, políticas educacionales y
culturales : Informe de Gestión 1990-1993.* Santiago: Ministerio de Educación, enero 1993.

Chili (suite) / Chile (continued)

4. Situation des bibliothèques scolaires et des centres documentaires scolaires
Situation of School Libraries and Resource Centers

170. Faundez, Paola Violeta Garcia. *Las bibliotecas escolares en Chile.* 21 p. + 2 annexes. (paper given at the IFLA Pre-session seminar on School Librarianship : Issues for Developing Countries, Caldes de Montbui, Spain, August 15-20, 1993).

171. Naveillan de Molinare, Teresa, and Yolande Soto. *The current situation of school libraries in South America with special reference to Chile.* (paper given at the Open session of the Section of School Libraries, 53rd IFLA General Conference, Brighton, 1987).

5. Rapports et autres documents / Reports and Other Documents

172. Chile. Instituto Nacional de Estadísticas. *Anuario de cultura y medios de comunicación 1989-1990-1991-1992.* S.l. : Instituto Nacional de Estadísticas. Depto. de Estadísticas Demográficas, 1996.

Chine / China

2. Politiques, normes et lignes directrices en bibliothéconomie scolaire
Policies, Standards and Guidelines in School Librarianship

173. China. National Education Commission. *Rules for school libraries.* S.l. : National Education Commission, 1991.

4. Situation des bibliothèques scolaires et des centres documentaires scolaires
Situation of School Libraries and Resource Centers

174. Dong, Xiaoying, and Shuhua Zhang. *Report of School Libraries in China.* 6 p. (paper given at the IFLA Pre-session seminar on School Librarianship : Issues for Developing Countries, Caldes de Montbui, Spain, August 15-20, 1993).

175. Jia Xiaobin, Du Yunxiang, Si Aiqin, and Zhang Xiaoyan. *China's primary and secondary school libraries: their history, status quo and future,* In: Booklet 3: Libraries serving the general public, pp. 111-121. (paper given at the Open session of the Section of School Libraries, 62nd IFLA Conference, Beijing, China, August 25-31, 1996). (104-SCHOOL-2-E).

176. "The middle and primary school library regulation of the PRC." *University Library Journal* (1992).
Note: Enquête menée en 1994 par Galler (1996).

Colombie / Columbia

4. Situation des bibliothèques scolaires et des centres documentaires scolaires
Situation of School Libraries and Resource Centers

177. Isaza de Pedraza, Mary Luz. *Informe sobre las bibliotecas escolares en Colombia.* 5 p. (paper given at the IFLA Pre-session seminar on School Librarianship : Issues for Developing Countries, Caldes de Montbui, Spain, August 15-20, 1993).

Corée / Korea

4. *Situation des bibliothèques scolaires et des centres documentaires scolaires*
Situation of School Libraries and Resource Centers

178. Kim, Yong Won. *Current status of school libraries in Korea.* 18 p. (paper given at the 28th general conference of Japan School library Association, Fukuoka, Japan, July 29-31, 1992). Note: In Japanese.

Costa Rica

4. *Situation des bibliothèques scolaires et des centres documentaires scolaires*
Situation of School Libraries and Resource Centers

179. de Martinese, Reca, and Suzana Amalia. "Las bibliotecas escolares de Costa Rica." *Biblioteca escolar: un centro de aprendizaje* , no. 2/5, 1985, pp. 2-7.
Note: Éditeur de la revue / Editor of the journal: Argentina. Ministerio de Educación y justicia, secretaría de Educación. Subsecretaría de conducción educativa.

Cuba

2. *Politiques, normes et lignes directrices en bibliothéconomie scolaire*
Policies, Standards and Guidelines in School Librarianship

180. Cuba. Ministerio de Educación. "La Biblioteca escolar en el proceso docente educativo." En: *La asimilación del contenido de la enseñanza*, Por Mercedes Aguiar et al. Habana: Ed. Libros para la educación, 1979, pp. 101-102.

181. ___. *Reglamento de bibliotecas escolares : resolución ministerial No 729/80.* Habana: Ministerio de Educación, 1981, 19 p.

4. *Situation des bibliothèques scolaires et des centres documentaires scolaires*
Situation of School Libraries and Resource Centers

182. Chomat, Mercedes Alfonso, and Idelio Rojas Crespo. *La biblioteca escolar en Cuba : un recurso para la educación.* 13 p. + annexes I-V. (paper given at the Open session of the Section of the School Libraries, 60th IFLA Conference, La Habana, Cuba, August 21-27, 1994).

183. Urquhart., Felix. *The development of the school library system in Cuba,* (paper given at the Open session of the Section of the School Libraries, 60th IFLA Conference, Havana, Cuba, August 21-27 1994).

Danemark / Denmark

1. *Politiques générales d'éducation / General Educational Policies*

184. Denmark. Education Act on the Folkeskole. "Extract from the Education Act on the Kolkeskole." In: Danish Association of School Librarians; Danish Association of School Libraries. *School libraries in Denmark.* By Hanne Heiselberg, Niels Jacobsen and Inga Nielsen. Viby Zealand: The Danish Association of School Librarians, 1997, pp. 13-14.
Note: Published in Danish, English and German.

Danemark (suite) / Denmark (continued)

2. *Politiques, normes et lignes directrices en bibliothéconomie scolaire*
Policies, Standards and Guidelines in School Librarianship

185.   Danish Association of School Librarians; Danish Association of School Libraries. *School
     libraries in Denmark.* By Hanne Heiselberg, Niels Jacobsen and Inga Nielsen. Viby
     Zealand: The Danish Association of School Librarians, 1997. 16 p.
     Note: Published in Danish, English and German.

**3. *Lois, décrets et règlements en matière de bibliothèques et de centres
   documentaires scolaires***
   Laws, Decrees and Rules about School Libraries and Resource Centers

186.   Denmark. Danish public libraries act. *Ministerial order of the Ministry of cultural affairs no.
     658 of 14th december 1983, amendments of 10th May, 1989, of 26th June 1989, and of 15th
     January 1990*. Copenhagen : National Library Authority, 1991. 6 p.

187.   Denmark. Ministry of Education. Regulations on school libraries. In: Danish Association of
     School Librarians; Danish Association of School Libraries *School libraries in Denmark*. By
     Hanne Heiselberg, Niels Jacobsen and Inga Nielsen. Viby Zealand: The Danish Association
     of School Librarians, 1997, pp. 14-15.
     Note: Published in Danish, English and German.

188.   Petersen, Jes. "New trends within Danish school library legislation ." *Scandinavian Public
     Library Quarterly* , vol. 24, no. 2, 1991, pp. 4-5.
     Note: Cité par/citation by Galler (1996).

5. *Rapports et autres documents / Reports and Other Documents*

189.   Christensen, Jytte. *The difference and the likeness between the school library and the public
     library in Denmark.* (paper given at the Open session of the Section of the School Libraries,
     56th IFLA Conference, Stockholm, 1990).

190.   Harbo, Ole. "Education for librarianship in Denmark." *Liber bulletin* , vol. 27, 1986, pp. 31-32.

191.   Sorfensen, Birgit. *La collaboration entre bibliothèques publiques et bibliothèques scolaires au
     Danemark.* (communication au séminaire international sur la création de modèles de
     jumelages institutionnels pour les bibliothèques du Sud et du Nord, Banque internationale
     d'information sur les états francophones, Ottawa, 20-21 juin 1991).

El Salvador

2. *Politiques, normes et lignes directrices en bibliothéconomie scolaire*
Policies, Standards and Guidelines in School Librarianship

192.   El Salvador. Ministerio de Educación. Dirección Nacional de Educación. Dirreción de
     Materiales Educativos. *Red nacional de bibliotecas escolares, como centros de recursos
     par el aprendizaje.* Nueva San Salvador: 1994.
     Note: Enquête menée en 1994 par Galler (1996).

Espagne / Spain

1. *Politiques générales d'éducation / General Educational Policies*

193.   España. Ministerio de Educación y Ciencia. *Libro blanco para la reforma del sistema educativo.*
     Madrid: Ministerio de Educación y Ciencia, 1984. 379 p.

Espagne (suite) / Spain (continued)

2. *Politiques, normes et lignes directrices en bibliothéconomie scolaire*
Policies, Standards and Guidelines in School Librarianship

194. España. Ministerio de Educación y Cienca. *Un nuevo concepto de biblioteca escolar.* Madrid: 1996.
Note: Enquête menée en 1994 par Galler (1996).

195. España. Ministerio de Educación y Ciencia. *La biblioteca escolar en el contexto de la reforma educativa: documento marco.* Madrid: El Ministerio, 1995. 102 p.
Note de Ramon Salaberria: Document de base et lignes directrices d'un Programme de développement de bibliothèques scolaires et d'un projet pilote qui n'ont malheureusement pas pu voir le jour...

3. *Lois, décrets et règlements en matière de bibliothèques et de centres*
documentaires scolaires
Laws, Decrees and Rules about School Libraries and Resource Centers

196. "Bibliotecas de Castilla y Leon. Ley 9/1989, de 30 de noviembre." *Boletín Oficial del Estado-BOE* 23-1-90.
Note de Ramon Salaberria: Intègre les bibliothèques scolaires dans le système des bibliothèques et mentionne la collaboration entre différents types de bibliothèques.

197. "Bibliotecas de Castilla-La Mancha. Ley 1/1989, de 4 de mayo." *Boletín Oficial del Estado-BOE* , no. 142, (15/06/89) .
Note de Ramon Salaberria: Un article de cette loi régionale sur les bibliothèques traite de la collaboration entre les différentes bibliothèques, dont les bibliothèques scolaires.

198. Canarias. "Orden de 23 de mayo de 1990, por la que se autoriza el desarrollo del proyecto "Hipatia" para la organización y fomento del uso de las bibliotecas en las enseñanzas no universitarias, y se integra en el Programa de Innovación Educativa." *Boletín Oficial de Canarias,* 11/6/91.
Note de Ramon Salaberria: Programme pour le développement des bibliothèques scolaires dans les établissements de l'enseignement secondaire aux Canaries: prévu pour au moins cinq ans, mais arrête après la 2e année, faute de pouvoir créer sept postes de bibliothécaires pour gérer 30 bibliothèques scolaires.

199. Comunidad de Madrid. Consejería de Educación y Cultura, and Ministerio de Educación y Cultura de España. "Programa de Bibliotecas de Aula y Escolares.
Orden 448/1990, de 30 de noviembre (Boletín Oficial de la Comunidad de Madrid-BOCM, de 3 de diciembre); Orden 1053-E/1991, de 9 de octubre (BOCM de 16 de octubre); Orden 932/1992, de 16 de julio (BOCM de 21 de julio); Orden 741/1993, de 29 de junio (BOCM de 14 de julio) y Orden 992/1994, de 1 de octubre." *Boletín Oficial de la Comunidad Autónoma de Madrid de 1 de octubre*
Note de Ramon Salaberria: Programme important visant a aménager des "coins lecture" et des bibliothèques scolaires dès le préscolaire; a duré 5 années, de 1990-91 à 1994-95 et a touché 764 centres éducatifs, soit 90,4% du total; budget total: 430,5 millions de pesetas). Note: Pour en savoir plus: Educación y Biblioteca. no. 55, marzo 1995 (numéro spécial sur les bibliothèques publiques et scolaires de la région de Madrid).

200. España. "Real Decreto 1004/1991, 14 de junio, por el que se establecen los requisitos mínimos de los Centros que imparten enseñanzas de régimen general no universitarias." *Boletín Oficial del Estado-BOE.* no 152, 26/6/1991 .
Note de Ramon Salaberria: Décret royal sur les conditions minimales que doivent remplir les établissements d'enseignement; prévoit en particulier l'espace en mètres carrés à réserver aux bibliothèques: 45 m2 pour les écoles, 60 pour les collèges, 75 pour les lycées et 60 pour les lycées techniques.

Espagne (suite) / Spain (continued)

3. Lois, décrets et règlements en matière de bibliothèques et de centres documentaires scolaires (suite)
Laws, Decrees and Rules about School Libraries and Resource Centers (continued)

201. España. Ministerio de Educación y Ciencia. *Orden de 29 de junio de 1994, por la que se aprueban las instrucciones que regulan la organización y el funcionamiento de los Institutos de Educación Secundaria. Boletín Oficial del Estado-BOE, no 159, 5/7/94 + Orden de 29 de junio de 1994, por la que se aprueban las instrucciones que regulan la organización y el funcionamiento de las Escuelas de Educación Infantil y de los Colegios de Educación Primaria. Boletín Oficial del Estado-BOE, no 160, 6/7/94.*
Note de Ramon Salaberria: Ces deux règlements précisent les caractéristiques du professeur responsable de la bibliothèque scolaire, son horaire et ses fonctions. La bibliothèque fait partie des "activités complémentaires et extrascolaires".

202. Galicia. "Bibliotecas. Ley 14/1989, de 11 de octubre." *Boletín Oficial del Estado-BOE , no 35, 9/2/90.*
Note de Ramon Salaberria: Signale l'importance des bibliothèques scolaires et ouvre la possibilité de créer des bibliothèques à double usage, public et scolaire.

203. Organización Bibliotecaria de la Comunidad Valenciana. "Ley 10/1986, 30 de diciembre." *Boletín Oficial del Estado-BOE , no. 30, de 13/02/8*
Note de Ramon Salaberria: Encourage la création et/ou le développement de bibliothèques scolaires.

204. Sistema bibliotecario de Cataluña. "Ley 4/1993 de 18 de marzo." *Boletín Oficial del Estado-BOE. 21/4/93.*
Note de Ramon Salaberria: Points importants: les bibliothèques scolaires font partie du Système des bibliothèques de la Catalogne; identifie les fonctions de la bibliothèque scolaire: fournit des ressources que l'élève peut intégrer à ses apprentissages, facilite l'accès à la culture, enseigne aux élèves l'utilisation du fonds documentaire, et participe à la formation et aux loisirs de l'élève; aborde la question de la coordination entre les bibliothèques publiques et bibliothèques scolaires.

4. Situation des bibliothèques scolaires et des centres documentaires scolaires
Situation of School Libraries and Resource Centers

205. Baro, Mónica, Teresa Manà, and Anna M. Roig. *Les biblioteques a les escoles publiques a Catalunya.* Barcelona : Diputacio de Barcelona, 1990. 79 p.

206. Baro, Mónica and Teresa Manà. *Aproximación al estado actual de las bibliotecas escolares en España.* 10 p. (paper given at the IFLA Pre-session seminar on School Librarianship : Issues for Developing Countries, Caldes de Montbui, Spain, August 15-20, 1993).

Estonie / Estonia

2. Politiques, normes et lignes directrices en bibliothéconomie scolaire
Policies, Standards and Guidelines in School Librarianship

207. Esthonia. Ministry of Culture and Education. *Resolution no. 4. Approval Of School Library Statutes.* Tallin: 1995.
Note: Enquête menée en 1994 par Galler (1996).

4. Situation des bibliothèques scolaires et des centres documentaires scolaires
Situation of School Libraries and Resource Centers

208. Raatma, Irma. *Views of estonian school libraries.* 8 p. + 1 tabl. (paper given at the IFLA Pre-session seminar on School Librarianship : Issues for Developing Countries, Caldes de Montbui, Spain, August 15-20, 1993).

États-Unis / United States of America

2. Politiques, normes et lignes directrices en bibliothéconomie scolaire
Policies, Standards and Guidelines in School Librarianship

209. American Association of School Librarians. *Curriculum folio guidelines for the NCATE review process : school library media specialist : basic preparation.* Chicago, Ill. : American Library Association, 1989. 47 p.

210. ___. *Educational excellence through effective school library media programs.* Chicago, Ill. : American Library Association, 1989. 14 p.

211. American Association of School Librarians; Association for Educational Communications and Technology. *Information power: guidelines for school library media programs.* Chicago, Ill. : American Library Association, 1988. XI-171 p.

212. American Library Association. *Presidential commission on information literacy : Final report .* Chicago, Ill. : ALA, 1989. 17 p.

213. Cleaver, B. P. and W. D. Taylor. *The instructional consultant role of the school library media specialist.* Chicago : American Library Association, 1988.

214. Marcoux, Betty and Delia Neumann. "Into the twenty-first century : new guidelines and standards for library media programs." *School library media quarterly ,* vol. 24, no. 4, Summer 1996, pp. 213-216.

215. Mellon, Constance A., and Emily S. Boyce. "School library standards : a force for change in library services for children and young adults." *Journal of youth services in libraries ,* vol. 6, no. 2, Winter 1993, pp. 128-138.

216. Rooke, Jill. "National school library standards / guidelines post-world war II to the present." *Indiana media journal ,* vol. 12, no. 3. Spring 1990, pp. 22-30.

217. Vandergrift, Kay E., and Jane A. Hannigan. "Elementary school library media centers as essential components in the schooling process : an AASL position paper." *School library media quarterly ,* vol. 14, no. 4, Summer 1986, pp. 171-173.

<u>Documents des différents états / Documents from differents States</u>

218. Colorado. State Library and Adult Education Office. *Model information literacy standards.* Denver, Colo. : State Library and Adult Education Office, Colorado Department of Education, 1994.

219. ___. *Information literacy guidelines.* Denver, Colo. : State Library and Adult Education Office, Colorado Department of Education, Colorado Educational Media Association, 1994.

220. Florida Department of Education. *Study guide for the Florida teacher certification examination : educational media specialist PK-12.* Tampa, Fla. : University of South Florida, College of Education, Institute for Instructional Research and Practice, 1989. 36 p.

221. Nevada. Department of Education. *Information power Nevada 1995 : Library media center standards.* Carson City, Nev. : The Department, 1995. 72 p.

222. New York. State Education Department. *A new compact for learning. A partnership to improve educational results in New York State.* Albany, N.Y. : The Department, 1991. 19 p.

223. Oklahoma State Department of Education. *PASS: Priority Academic Student Skills.* (Draft). Oklahoma City : the Department, Revised November 1996.
    Note: Draft for discussion and review only.

États-Unis (suite) / United States of America (continued)

2. Politiques, normes et lignes directrices en bibliothéconomie scolaire (suite)
Policies, Standards and Guidelines in School Librarianship (continued)

224. South Carolina Department of Education. *Focus on South Carolina School Library Media Programs. Making connections.* Columbia : The Department, 1996. 38 p.

225. Texas State Library. *School Library Services. Standards and guidelines for Texas.* Austin : The Library, 1/31/1997. 17 p.
    Note: Draft for discussion only.

226. Wisconsin Educational Media Association; Information Literacy Committee. *Information literacy : a position paper on information problem–solving.* Dir. by Carol J. Nelson. s.l. : WEMA, 1993. 4 p.

227. Wisconsin Library Association; Wisconsin School Library Association. *Wisconsin library and information skills guide,* Dir. by Mary G. Mickel. Madison, Wis. : WSLA, 1992. 113 p.

3. Lois, décrets et règlements en matière de bibliothèques et de centres documentaires scolaires
Laws, Decrees and Rules about School Libraries and Resource Centers

228. Hopkins, D. McAfee and R. Butler. *The federal roles in support of school library media centers.* Chicago, Ill. : American Library Association, 1991. 185 p.

229. United States. *Elementary and secondary school library media act. Excerpt from the Congressional record .* Washington : American Library Association, 1992. 5 p.

4. Situation des bibliothèques scolaires et des centres documentaires scolaires
Situation of School Libraries and Resource Centers

230. Pritchett, Pamela P. "State agency reports." *School library media annual ,* vol. 9, 1991. p. 209.

5. Rapports et autres documents / Reports and Other Documents

231. Fitzgibbons, Shirley and Daniel Callison. "Research needs and issues in school librarianship." In: *Library and information science research: perspectives and strategies for improvement.* Charles R. McClure and Peter Hernon (Ed.)., Norwood, N.J. : Ablex, 1991, pp. 296-315.

232. Krashen, Stephen D. *Power of reading. Insights from the research.* Englewood, CO : Libraries Unlimited, 1993. 120 p.

233. Lance, Keith Curry, Lynda Welborn and Christine Hamilton-Pennell. *Impact of school library media centers on academic achievement.* Castle Rock, CO : Hi Willow Research and Publishing, 1993. 144 p.

234. Mathews, Virginia H. *Kids can't wait... Library advocacy now!,* A President's paper. Chicago : American Library Association. 20 p. + 6 p. (pamphlet).

235. Mathews, Virginia H., Judith G. Flum and Karen A. Whitney. "Kids need libraries. School and public libraries preparing the youth of today for the world of tomorrow."*School library journal ,* vol. 36, no. 4, April 1990, pp. 33-37.

236. Perritt, Patsy H. "School library media certification requirements : 1990 update." *School library journal ,* vol. 36, no. 6, June 1990, pp. 41-61.

237. Stripling, Barbara K. *Libraries for the national education goals.* Syracuse. N.Y. : ERIC Clearinghouse on Information resources, Syracuse University, 1992. II-118 p. (IR; 94).

États-Unis (suite) / United States of America (continued)

5. *Rapports et autres documents (suite) / Reports and Other Documents (continued)*

238.   Tryneski, John. *Requirements for certification of teachers, counselors, librarians, administrators for elementary and secondary schools 1990-1991.* 55th ed. Chicago, Ill. : The University of Chicago Press, 1990. 242 p.

Éthiopie / Ethiopia

**4. *Situation des bibliothèques scolaires et des centres documentaires scolaires*
*Situation of School Libraries and Resource Centers***

239.   Muhudien, Mohammed. *Ethiopia. Country Report.* 7 p. (paper given at the IFLA Pre-session seminar on School Librarianship : Issues for Developing Countries, Caldes de Montbui, Spain, August 15-20, 1993).

Finlande / Finland

**4. *Situation des bibliothèques scolaires et des centres documentaires scolaires*
*Situation of School Libraries and Resource Centers***

240.   Haapsaari, Raija. "School libraries in Finland." *Scandinavian public library quarterly* , vol. 29, 1991, pp. 15-20.

5. *Rapports et autres documents / Reports and Other Documents*

241.   Niinikangas, Liisa. "An open learning environment - new winds in the Finnish school library." *Scandinavian public library quarterly* , no. 4, 1995, pp. 4-10.

France

**2. *Politiques, normes et lignes directrices en bibliothéconomie scolaire*
*Policies, Standards and Guidelines in School Librarianship***

242.   France. Ministère de l'Éducation. "Mission des personnels exerçant dans les centres de documentation et d'information." *Bulletin Officiel* , no. 12, 27 mars 1986.
        Note: Circulaire no 86-123 du 13 mars 1986.

243.   Jospin, Lionel. "Discours du ministre de l'Éducation nationale, de la Jeunesse et des Sports prononcé à Arras le 23 mars 1989 sur la réussite scolaire pour tous les élèves, les zones d'éducation prioritaires et la maîtrise du langage." *Bulletin Officiel* , no. 15, 13 avril 1989, pp. 897-902.

244.   Poupelin, Michel et Marie Monthus. *Guide à l'usage des documentalistes et de leurs partenaires dans l'établissement.* Paris : CNDP; Hachette, 1993. 125 p.

245.   "Spécial métier 1." *Médiadoc* , juin 1995. 40 p.
        Note: (Numéro thématique du bulletin de la Fédération des enseignants documentalistes de l'Éducation nationale/FADBEN).

246.   "Spécial métier 2." *Médiadoc* , décembre 1995. 36 p.
        Note: (Numéro thématique du bulletin de la Fédération des enseignants documentalistes de l'Éducation nationale/FADBEN).

France (suite / continued)

2. *Politiques, normes et lignes directrices en bibliothéconomie scolaire (suite)*
Policies, Standards and Guidelines in School Librarianship (continued)

247. "Spécial métier 3." *Médiadoc*, mai 1996. 32 p.
Note: (Numéro thématique du bulletin de la Fédération des enseignants documentalistes de l'Éducation nationale/FADBEN).

3. *Lois, décrets et règlements en matière de bibliothèques et de centres documentaires scolaires*
Laws, Decrees and Rules about School Libraries and Resource Centers

248. France. Ministère de l'Éducation. "Loi d'orientation sur l'éducation." *Bulletin Officiel* , no. 4 (spécial), 31 août 1989.
Note: Concerne l'engagement du ministère de l'Éducation nationale, de la Jeunesse et des Sports de doter d'un poste de documentaliste tout établissement du second degré qui ouvre ses portes.

4. *Situation des bibliothèques scolaires et des centres documentaires scolaires*
Situation of School Libraries and Resource Centers

249. *Diagnostic et prospective d'une profession : 1er Congrès des documentalistes de lycées et collèges, Strasbourg, 21 mai 1989.* . Paris : Nathan, 1990. 96 p.

250. "Évaluation des CDI par l'Inspection générale, 1994." *Inter CDI* , no. 137, septembre-octobre 1995.

251. France. Ministère de l'Éducation. *Rapport de l'Inspection générale de l'Éducation nationale 1994.* Paris : Documentation française, 1994.

252. Parent, Yves. *L'histoire des bibliothèques scolaires en France : évolutions et perspectives actuelles.* 7 p. (Présentation à la session publique de la section des bibliothèques scolaires, 55e Conférence générale et Congrès de l'IFLA, Paris, 23 août 1989).

253. Privat, Jean-Marie. *Bibliothèque. école : quelles coopérations ? Rapport d'enquête. Actes de l'Université d'été de La Grande-Motte, 26-29 octobre 1993...* . Créteil, France : CRDP d'Ile-de-France, Académie de Créteil, 1994. 271 p. (Collection Argos).

5. *Rapports et autres documents / Reports and Other Documents*

254. Bayard-Pierlot, Jacqueline et Marie-José Birglin. *Le CDI au coeur du projet pédagogique.* Paris : Hachette Éducation, 1991.

255. Butlen, Max, Madeleine Couet et Lucie Desailly. *Savoir lire avec les bibliothèques centres documentaires.* Préf. de Jean Hébrard. Le Perreux : CRDP de l'Académie de Créteil, 1996. 290 p.

256. Chapron, Françoise. *Documentation, Information, Éducation: Bibliographie sélective.* Paris : FADBEN/CDI, 1996. 54 p. (Collection MÉDIADOC).

257. Chapron, Françoise et François Roux. "Enseignants en documentation ou documentalistes enseignants?" *Documentaliste-sciences de l'information* , vol. 27, no. 4-5, 1990, pp. 227-229.

258. Chapron, Françoise et Michel Treut. *Proposition pour la formation des documentalistes-bibliothécaires des CDI des lycées et collèges,* : séminaire organisé par la FADBEN les 6 et 7 octobre 1989 à Paris. Dossier. Paris : Fédération des Associations de documentalistes-bibliothécaires de l'Education nationale, 1990, 35 p. (MÉDIADOC FADBEN dossiers).

88

France (suite / continued)

5. *Rapports et autres documents (suite) / Reports and Other Documents (continued)*

259. Charrier, Colette. *Le CDI, outil pédagogique des enseignants pour une mise en place d'une formation à l'information en équipe professeur-documentaliste.* In: Booklet 3: Libraires serving the general public, pp. 122-129. (paper given at the Open session of the Section of School Libraries, 62nd IFLA Conference, Beijing, China, August 25-31, 1996). (008-SCHOOL-1-F).

260. "Continuité et ruptures: bibliothèques et centres documentaires de la maternelle à l'université." *Argos*, no. 14, mars 1995.

261. "La documentation, un outil pour toute une équipe." *Cahiers pédagogiques*, no. 332-333, mars-avril 1995.

262. Estela-Garcia, Annie et Nicole Rivallain. *Travailler au CDI en histoire-géographie.* Paris : Hachette Éducation, 1994.

263. France. Ministère de l'Éducation nationale. Groupe de travail national sur les seconds cycles. *Les lycéens et leurs études au seuil du XXIe siècle. Rapport du Groupe de travail national sur les seconds cycles présidé par M. Antoine Prost.* Paris: Centre national de documentation pédagogique, 1983. 288 p.

264. Gaillot, Ph. et R. Gaillot. *Et si on travaillait avec notre documentaliste!*. Tours, France : CDDP, 1993.

265. Hassenforder, Jean et Odile Chesnot-Lambert. "Les expériences de l'ADACES : essai d'évaluation." *Médiathèques publiques*, no. 56, octobre-décembre 1980, pp. 17-28.

266. Héraud, Brigitte. *Les bibliothèques centres documentaires.* Paris : Centre national de documentation pédagogique, Service central de ressources documentaires, 1987. (Collection Guides documentaires).

267. IUFM de Poitiers OAVUP. *Apprendre au CDI,* : IUFM/OAVUP, 1995. 1 vidéocassette VHS, 21 min.

268. Leblond, Françoise. *Les nouveaux documentalistes.* Paris: Ellipses, 1994.

269. *Méthodes et techniques pour travailler au CDI et en classe, 1er cycle*. Angers, France : CRDP, 1993.

270. Mollard, Michèle. *Les CDI à l'heure du management.* Villeurbanne, France : Services des publications, 1996. 184 p.

271. Morizio, Claude, Marie-Paule Saj et Michel Souchaud. *Les technologies de l'information au CDI.* Paris : Hachette, 1996. 192 p. (Hachette Éducation).

272. Murail, Marie-Aude. *Continue la lecture, on n'aime pas la récré...*. Paris: Calman-Lévy, 1993. 185 p.

273. *Pour une pédagogie documentaire: expériences de recherche documentaire au collège.* Paris : Ministère de l'Éducation nationale , 1994.

274. *Quel profil professionnel pour les documentalistes des CDI des établissements scolaires du second degré?* Séminaire organisé par la FADBEN, les 9-10 novembre 1995 à Paris. Rouen : FADBEN, s.d., 35 p. + annexes. (Médiadoc. Dossiers).

275. Righi, Dominique. *Animer une BCD.* Paris : Hachette, 1993.

276. ___. *Une BCD pour lire et écrire.* Paris : Hachette, 1993.

France (suite / continued)

5. *Rapports et autres documents (suite) / Reports and Other Documents (continued)*

277.   "Se documenter." *Argos* , no. 9, 1992.

278.   "S'informer, se documenter." *Innovations* , 1992, no. 25-26.

279.   Vernotte, France. "Enseignants documentalistes: un métier en question." *Bulletin des bibliothèques de France* , vol. 40, no. 6, novembre 1995,   pp. 72-76.

280.   ___. *Les bibliothèques scolaires comme outil de formation à l'information du citoyen de l'an 2000. L'exemple français: les CDI des établissements scolaires.*   In: Booklet 3: Libraries serving the general public, pp. 90-95. (paper given at the Open session of the Section of the School Libraries, 61st IFLA Conference, Istanbul, August 20-26, 1995). (080-SCHOOL-3-F).

Ghana

4. *Situation des bibliothèques scolaires et des centres documentaires scolaires*
Situation of School Libraries and Resource Centers

281.   Osei-Bonsu, Moses. "Secondary school libraries in Ghana: a evaluative study." *International review of children's literature and librarianship* , vol. 5, no. 2, 1990,   pp. 87-104.

Hongrie / Hungary

2. *Politiques, normes et lignes directrices en bibliothéconomie scolaire*
Policies, Standards and Guidelines in School Librarianship

282.   Celler, Zsuzsanna. *Az iskolai könyvtàrak müködési normài. (Guidelines for the functioning of school libraries).* 1993.
Note: Enquête menée en 1994 par Galler (1996).

283.   Hungary. Ministry of Education and Culture. *Guidelines of the Hungarian Ministry of Education and Culture on the development of school libraries.* The Ministry, 1987.
Note: A reference not the real citation to the existence of the guidelines.

4. *Situation des bibliothèques scolaires et des centres documentaires scolaires*
Situation of School Libraries and Resource Centers

284.   Celler, Zsuzsanna. "School libraries in Hungary." 5 p. + 1 tabl. (paper given at the IFLA Pre-session seminar on School librarianship : Issues for Developing Countries, Caldes de Montbui, Spain, August 15-20, 1993).

5. *Rapports et autres documents / Reports and Other Documents*

285.   Celler, Zsuzsanna. "Literacy, literature and learning in school libraries in Hungary." In: *Booklet 3* : Division of libraries serving the general public, pp. 16-18. (paper given at the Open session of the Section of the School Libraries, 59th IFLA Council and General Conference, Barcelona, Spain, August 22-28, 1993).

Iles Fidji / Fiji

2. Politiques, normes et lignes directrices en bibliothéconomie scolaire
Policies, Standards and Guidelines in School Librarianship

286.   Prasad, Humesh. "Development of standards for school libraries in Fiji : a paper presented at the Bi-annual Convention of the Fiji Library Association held on 5th December, 1992 at the Institute of Social and Administration Studies, University of the South Pacific, Suva, Fiji." *Fiji library association journal* , no. 29, (June 1993), pp. 21-28.

4. Situation des bibliothèques scolaires et des centres documentaires scolaires
Situation of School Libraries and Resource Centers

287.   Prasad, Humesh. "Fiji school library services in Fiji : Country Paper." 12 p. + 1 carte. (paper given at the IFLA Pre-session seminar on School Librarianship : Issues for Developing Countries, Caldes de Montbui, Spain, August 15-20, 1993).

5. Rapports et autres documents / Reports and Other Documents

288.   Rainey, Melvyn. "School libraries in Fiji." *Australian library review* , vol. 9, no. 3, August 1992, pp. 199-208.

Inde / India

3. Lois, décrets et règlements en matière de bibliothèques et de centres documentaires scolaires
Laws, Decrees and Rules about School Libraries and Resource Centers

289.   ""Delhi School Education Act 1973." In: *Proceedings of the all India seminar on school library development, New Delhi, 19-20 September, 1986."* ILA Bulletin, vol. 1-2, no. 22, April-September 1986, pp. 87-94.

4. Situation des bibliothèques scolaires et des centres documentaires scolaires
Situation of School Libraries and Resource Centers

290.   Powdwal, Sushama. *School libraries in India : a country report.* 14 p. + 3 annexes. (paper given at the IFLA Pre-session seminar on School Librarianship : Issues for Developing Countries, Caldes de Montbui, Spain, August 15-20, 1993).

5. Rapports et autres documents / Reports and Other Documents

291.   Sahni, Neera. *School libraries in developed countries and adoption of their techniques in a developing country like India .* 8 p. + 4 p. annexes.
Note: Paper based on a study undertaken in Netherlands and Germany (...) under the "Gustav Hofman Study Grant - 1992" awarded by IFLA.

Indonésie / Indonesia

1. Politiques générales d'éducation / General Educational Policies

292.   Asean Committee on Culture and Information. *Introduction to Asean librarianship: school libraries.* Ed. by S. Soekarman and S. Wardaya, Jakarta : National Library of Indonesia, 1992. 92 p.

Iran

5. Rapports et autres documents / Reports and Other Documents

293. Jowkar, A. and M. Kinnel. "Educating school librarians in Iran." *Libri*, vol. 43, no. 2, 1993, pp. 91-107.

Islande / Iceland

4. Situation des bibliothèques scolaires et des centres documentaires scolaires
Situation of School Libraries and Resource Centers

294. Hannesdóttir, Sigrún Klara. "Survey of elementary school libraries in Iceland 1989-1990." *Scandinavian public library quarterly*, no. 2, 1991, pp. 9-14.

295. ___. "National survey of primary school libraries in Iceland." *Australian library review*, vol. 9, no. 3, August 1992, pp. 187-198.

296. ___. "School library development in Iceland." (paper given at the16th annual Conference of the International Association of School Librarianship, Reykjavik, Iceland, July 26-31, 1989).

297. ___. *Brief information on school librarians and school library education in Iceland.*, October 1991, 2 p.

Israël / Israel

2. Politiques, normes et lignes directrices en bibliothéconomie scolaire
Policies, Standards and Guidelines in School Librarianship

298. *The library - a resource centre in primary and secondary schools.*
Note: (In Hebrew). Program for library management. Schools. Instructions for purchasing materials. The library a-resource centre. Enquête menée en 1994 par Galler (1996).

3. Lois, décrets et règlements en matière de bibliothèques et de centres documentaires scolaires
Laws, Decrees and Rules about School Libraries and Resource Centers

299. Israel. Ministry of Education. *The Library Department.* (translated from Hebrew). 6 p.
Note: Received in March 1997 from the Library Department, Ministry of Education.

4. Situation des bibliothèques scolaires et des centres documentaires scolaires
Situation of School Libraries and Resource Centers

300. Israel. Ministry of Education. *A survey of school libraries 1993-1994* . (translated from Hebrew). 7 p.
Note: Received in March 1997 from the Library Department, Ministry of Education.

92

Israël (suite) / Israel (continued)

4. Situation des bibliothèques scolaires et des centres documentaires scolaires (suite)
Situation of School Libraries and Resource Centers (continued)

301.   Yitzhaki, Moshe, and Snunith Shoham. "An analysis of secondary school libraries in Israel." *International Library Review* , vol. 22, no. 4, December 1990, pp. 239-249.

Italie / Italia

1. Politiques générales d'éducation / General Educational Policies

302.   Cavallieri, Marina. "L'Italie revoit la copie de l'école; Le monde de l'éducation, de la culture et de la formation." *Courrier international* , no. 246, mars 1997, pp. 90-91.

2. Politiques, normes et lignes directrices en bibliothéconomie scolaire
Policies, Standards and Guidelines in School Librarianship

303.   Carroll, Frances Laverne. *Linee guida per le biblioteche scolastiche.* Roma : Associazione Biblioteche, 1995, 34 p. (Rapporti AIB 5).
Note: Traduction du document publié par l'IFLA en 1990/translation of the 1990 IFLA publication : *Guidelines for school libraries.*

Jamaïque / Jamaica

1. Politiques générales d'éducation / General Educational Policies

304.   Jamaica. Ministry of Education and Culture. Core Curriculum Unit. *Reform of secondary education: a summary document.* Kingston : The Ministry, 1993.

305.   Jamaica. Ministry of Education and Culture. Planning and Development Unit. *School mapping and micro-planning in education project Jam/83/011.* Kingston : The Ministry, Planning and Development Unit, 1990.

306.   ___. *Improvement and expansion of primary education : inter-american development. Bank phase two.* Kingston : The Ministry, Planning and Development Unit, 1990.

2. Politiques, normes et lignes directrices en bibliothéconomie scolaire
Policies, Standards and Guidelines in School Librarianship

307.   Library Association, and Commonwealth Library Association. *Policy guidelines for school library development in the Caribbean.* Comp. by Katie M. Mungho and Amy Robertson. Kingston: Jamaica Library Service, 1986. 29 p.

4. Situation des bibliothèques scolaires et des centres documentaires scolaires
Situation of School Libraries and Resource Centers

308.   Anderson, Beatrice L. "School libraries in Jamaica. A short report". 11 p. (paper given at the IFLA Pre-session seminar on School Librarianship : Issues for Developing Countries, Caldes de Montbui, Spain, August 15-20, 1993).

309.   Marshall, Eileen. "School libraries : programs and personnel." *Jamaica library association bulletin,* 1991/92. pp. 7-12.

Jamaïque (suite) / Jamaica (continued)

5. *Rapports et autres documents / Reports and Other Documents*

310. Jamaica. University of West Indies. *School library as a learning resource Centre. A course for teacher–librarians.* Mona, Jamaica : University of West Indies, 2 vol., 220 + 275 p., 1989.
Note: Vol. 1, Presenter's guide. / Vol. 2, Participant's text.

311. Knuth, Rebecca. "The impact of an international professional organization on school librarianship in Jamaica." *Third world libraries* , vol. 6, no. 2, 1996, pp. 36-52.

312. Lampart, Sheila L. "Twinning of libraries : objectives relating to public, school and university libraries." In: *Actes du Séminaire international sur la création de modèles de jumelages institutionnels à l'intention des bibliothèques du Sud et du Nord, Ottawa, 20-21 juin 1991.*, Ottawa : Banque internationale d'information sur les états francophones, 1991, pp. 31-35.
Note: Document émanant du National Council on Libraries, Archives and Information Systems (NACOLAIS, Jamaica).
Version en français: *Le jumelage des bibliothèques : objectifs pour les bibliothèques publiques, scolaires et universitaires.* 5 p.

Japon / Japan

2. *Politiques, normes et lignes directrices en bibliothéconomie scolaire*
Policies, Standards and Guidelines in School Librarianship

313. *A white paper of school libraries*, S.l. : Japan School Library Association, 1983. 219 p.
Note: In Japanese.

314. *A white paper of school libraries 2*, S.l. : Japan School Library Association, 1990. 223 p.
Note: In Japanese.

3. *Lois, décrets et règlements en matière de bibliothèques et de centres documentaires scolaires*
Laws, Decrees and Rules about School Libraries and Resource Centers

315. "School libraries hightlighted in Government's policy." *National diet library newsletter* , no. 91, October 1993, p. 10.
Note: In English.

316. Yano, Kazuhiko. "Ministry of Education policy for the improvement of the school library." *Education and information* , no. 450, September 1995, pp. 26-29.
Note: In Japanese.

4. *Situation des bibliothèques scolaires et des centres documentaires scolaires*
Situation of School Libraries and Resource Centers

317. "School libraries." In: *Librarianship in Japan.* Revised ed. Ed. by International Relations Committee of Japan Library Association, Tokyo : Japan Library Association, 1994, pp. 49-56.

5. *Rapports et autres documents / Reports and Other Documents*

318. Horikawa, Teruyo. *The types and levels of the cooperation with teachers in the high school libraries in Japan.* 10 p. (paper given at the Open session of the Section of the School Libraries, 62nd IFLA Conference, Beijing, China, August 25-31 1996).

319. Koyama, Ikuko. *The guidance of reading and information skills in school libraries: Japan's case.* (paper given at the Open session of the Section of School Libraries, 52nd IFLA Conference, Tokyo, 1986). (106-SCHO-3-E).

Japon (suite) / Japan (continued)

5. *Rapports et autres documents (suite) / Reports and Other Documents (continued)*

320. Sagae, Ikuko. *A report from the Tokyo Association of High School Teacher Librarians.* 8 p.
(paper given at the 20th conference of the International Association of School Librarianship,
Everett, Washington, (U.S.), July 23-27, 1991).
Note: In English.

321. "A survey of school libraries and reading guidance." *Gakko toshokan*, no. 542, December 1995,
pp. 38-46.
Note: In Japanese.

Jordanie / Jordan

4. *Situation des bibliothèques scolaires et des centres documentaires scolaires*
Situation of School Libraries and Resource Centers

322. Ali, Muhaimad S. S. *Secondary school libraries in Jordan.* Amman, Jordan : Jordan Library
Association, 1989.

323. Faseh, Mary. *Jordan : Country Report.* 4 p. (paper given at the IFLA Pre-session seminar on
School Librarianship : Issues for Developing Countries, Caldes de Montbui, Spain, August
15-20, 1993).

Kazakstan

1. *Politiques générales d'éducation / General Educational Policies*

324. Kazakstan. Ministry of Education. Republic scientific pedagogical library. *Statute of the
secondary school library.* 1995. 7 p.
Note: Document in Kazakstan language. Enquête menée en 1994 par Galler (1996).

Kenya

4. *Situation des bibliothèques scolaires et des centres documentaires scolaires*
Situation of School Libraries and Resource Centers

325. Mukuvi, Michael K. "The current state of school libraries in Kenya: problems and prospects."
Information trends news magazine , vol. 3, no. 1, February 1990, pp. 45-54.

Liban / Lebanon

4. *Situation des bibliothèques scolaires et des centres documentaires scolaires*
Situation of School Libraries and Resource Centers

326. Kaidbey, Leila Hassan. *School library in Lebanon.* 5 p. + 4 p. annexes. (paper given at the
IFLA Pre-session seminar on School Librarianship : Issues for Developing Countries,
Caldes de Montbui, Spain, August 15-20, 1993).

Malaisie / Malaysia

1. Politiques générales d'éducation / General Educational Policies

327. Singh, Diljit. *Malaysia : Country report*. 5 p. (paper given at the IFLA Pre-session seminar on School Librarianship : Issues for Developing Countries, Caldes de Montbui, Spain, August 15-20, 1993).

4. Situation des bibliothèques scolaires et des centres documentaires scolaires
Situation of School Libraries and Resource Centers

328. Vias, Rita. *Establishing school resource centers: the Malaysian experience*. (paper given at the 18th annual Conference of the International Association of School Librarianship, Malaysia, July 22-26, 1989).

5. Rapports et autres documents / Reports and Other Documents

329. Singh, Diljit. *The Teacher's Activity Centres of Malaysia*. 13 p. (paper given at the 25th annual conference of the International Association of School librarianship, Ocho Rios, Jamaica, 1996).

330. Yaacob, Raja Abdullah, and Norma Abur Seman. *Toward achieving a critical thinking society in Malaysia : a challenge to school libraries and education systems*. (paper given at the 22nd annual Conference of the International Association of School Librarianship, Adelaide, South Australia, September 27-30, 1993).

Mexique / Mexico

2. Politiques, normes et lignes directrices en bibliothéconomie scolaire
Policies, Standards and Guidelines in School Librarianship

331. México. Secretaría de Educación Pública. *Programa para la Modernización Educativa 1989-1994*. México : Poder Ejecutivo Federa, 1989. 61 p.
Note de Ramon Salaberria: Mentionne la bibliothèque comme moyen pédagogique et propose de créer ou de développer des bibliothèques scolaires dans toutes les écoles primaires publiques. Cependant, la Ley General de Educacion adoptée en 1993 ne fait plus référence aux bibliothèques scolaires.

5. Rapports et autres documents / Reports and Other Documents

332. Dubovoy, Silvia. *La casa de los libros: módulo del conductor*. México : Consejo Nacional para la Cultura y las Artes, 1989. 70 p. (Leer es crecer).
Note de Ramon Salaberria: La maison des livres: guide du conducteur: un guide pratique pour la sélection, le catalogage et la classification de la collection; explications simples sur l'importance et le design d'une bibliothèque et du service de prêt.

333. ___. *El nino y los libros: manual teorico-practico*. México : Consejo Nacional para la Cultura y las Artes, 1989. 69 p. (Leer es crecer).
Note de Ramon Salaberria: L'enfant et les livres: manuel théorique-pratique.

Myanmar

4. Situation des bibliothèques scolaires et des centres documentaires scolaires
Situation of School Libraries and Resource Centers

334. Hla, Soe. *School libraries of Myanmar*. (paper given at the IFLA Pre-session seminar on School Librarianship : Issues for Developing Countries, Caldes de Montbui, Spain, August 15-20, 1993). 7 p.

Namibie / Namibia

2. *Politiques, normes et lignes directrices en bibliothéconomie scolaire*
Policies, Standards and Guidelines in School Librarianship

335. Republic of Namibia. Ministry of Education, Culture, Youth and Sport. Coordinating council sub-committee for library and information services in Namibia. *Long-term project proposals for school libraries.* Windhoek, Namibia : The Ministry, 1990.

4. *Situation des bibliothèques scolaires et des centres documentaires scolaires*
Situation of School Libraries and Resource Centers

336. Klynsmith, T. "School library/resource centre services in Namibia and coordination with teachers resource centres and local and foreign book provision aid projects." In: Tötemeyer, A-J.; Loubser J.; Marais, A. E. (Ed.). *Coordination of information systems and services in Namibia,* (papers of the seminar held in Windhoek, Namibia, February 25th to March, 5th 1993), Bonn: DSE, s.d., pp. 172-182.

337. Tötemeyer, A-J. "Legacy of the past: the state of school libraries in Namibia." *Information trends news magazine,* vol. 4, no. 1, February 1991, pp. 27-36.

338. ___. "Namibian school libraries : today and tomorrow." In: *School Library Conference proceedings.* Papers of the School library Conference Held at the University of Natal in Durban 23 to 26 June 1992. Pietermaritzburg, Natal : University of Natal, Department of Information Studies., pp. 30-35.

339. ___. "School libraries in Namibia." 12 p. + 9 p. annexes. (paper given at the IFLA Pre-session seminar on School Librarianship : Issues for Developing Countries, Caldes de Montbui, Spain, August 15-20, 1993).

340. Tötemeyer, A-J, and C. Stander. *The state of school libraries/media centres in Namibia and the need for training for school Libraries/media centres.* s.l. : University of Namibia, Department of Library and Information Science, 1992. 118 p.

Nigéria / Nigeria

1. *Politiques générales d'éducation / General Educational Policies*

341. Nigeria. Federal Ministry of Information. *National Policy on education,* Revised ed. Lagos : Federal Government Printer, 1981.

2. *Politiques, normes et lignes directrices en bibliothéconomie scolaire*
Policies, Standards and Guidelines in School Librarianship

342. Ogunsheye, F. A. *Manual for Nigerian School Libraries.* Ibabani Adadina Media Resource Centre, 1980.

343. Oyelekan, Gbadebo Oyeniran. "Planning school library with nomadic education scheme in Nigeria : a proposal." *Education libraries journal,* vol. 37, no. 1, Spring 1994, pp. 45-60.

4. *Situation des bibliothèques scolaires et des centres documentaires scolaires*
Situation of School Libraries and Resource Centers

344. Dike, Virginia W. "School Library Services in the 90's and Beyond." *Nigerian school library journal,* vol. 3, no. 1-2, 1993, pp. 6-16.

345. Jam, Zawua. "Centralized school library management system in Benue State." *The International Information and Library Review,* no. 24, 1992, pp. 253-268.

Nigéria (suite) / Nigeria (continued)

5. Rapports et autres documents / Reports and Other Documents

346. Dike, Virginia W. *Library resources in education.* Enugui, Nigeria : ABIC Publishers, 1993, 194 p.

347. ___. *Expanding educational horizons of Nigerian students.* 16 p. (paper given at the 25th annual conference of the International Association of School librarianship, Ocho Rios, Jamaica, 1996).

348. Fagbeja, Oladele. "Recent development in the provision and development of school libraries in schools in Nigeria (1985-1990)." *Education library journal*, vol. 36, no. 1, 1993, pp. 19-29.

349. Ogunleye, Gabriel Olubumi. "Manpower aspects of secondary school libraries in the 6-3-3-4 education system in Nigeria : the case of Ondo State." *Library review*, vol. 37, no. 4, 1988, pp. 28-34.

350. Shaibu, S. "Centralized/support service as a cost-effective way out of the school library chaos in Gongola State of Nigeria." *Education library journal*, vol. 33, no. 2, Summer 1990, pp. 23-33.

351. Umunnakwe, U. S. "The role of school libraries in Nigeria's New education policy." *Library review*, vol. 41, no. 4, 1992, pp. 49-54.

352. University of Ibadan. Abadina Media Resource Centre. *Effects of library use education programme on academic achievement and social development of the primary school child.* Ed. by F. Adetownn Ogunsheye. Ibadan, Nigeria : University of Ibadan, AMRC, 1987, 129 p.

Norvège / Norway

1. Politiques générales d'éducation / General Educational Policies

353. Kirke-, utdannings- og forskningsdepartementet. *Om prinsipper og retningslinjer for 10-erig grunnskoleny lfreplan. ISt.mexd. ; 29 (1994-95) (Principles and guidelines for 10 years of elementary schooling, new national plan).* Oslo: Departementet, 1995. - 54 s.

354. ___. *"Vi sme en alen lange..." ("Small children one foot high...").* Oslo: The Department, 1993. 92 p. St. melding nr. 40 (1992-93).

355. ___. *Skolebiblioteket og Skolereformene. St. prp ur. I (1994-5) (The school libraries and the educational reforms).*

356. *"Ny Lovgivning om opplfring" Nou 1995:18. (New educational laws).* Oslo: Statens forvaltningst-jeneste, 1995. 430 p. diagrams.

357. *St. meld nr 29 (1994-1995). Om prinsipper og retningslinjer for 10 å-riggrunnskole - ny læreplan.* Note: A new educational Reform for the whole school system, both primary (R97) and lower secondary education (R94). Note: Text only in Norwegian.

2. Politiques, normes et lignes directrices en bibliothéconomie scolaire
Policies, Standards and Guidelines in School Librarianship

358. Andresen, Åse Foss, Bror v. Krogh, Kirsten Leth Nielsen, and Charlotte Qvist. *Brukeropplæring i bibliotek i vidergående skole (User education in secondary high school).* Oslo : Norsk Bibliotekforening, 1996. 48 p.

98

2. Politiques, normes et lignes directrices en bibliothéconomie scolaire (suite)
Policies, Standards and Guidelines in School Librarianship (continued)

359. Elle, melle... Hvem far en god utdanning i Norge i dag ? (One, two, three... who will have a good education in Norway today?) . Oslo : Norsk Bibliotekforening, 1994. 12 p.

360. Kjekstad, Torny. Outline of the Norwegian guidelines for schools libraries. 4 p. (paper given at the Open session of the Section of School Libraries, 60th IFLA Conference, La Habana, Cuba, 21-27 August, 1994).

361. Norwegian Directorate for Public Libraries. Guidelines for cooperation between public and school libraries, Acknowledged by the Ministry of Culture 22.06.1995 in accordance with the Public Library Act of 20th December 1985.
Note: Texte disponible en norvégien uniquement pour le moment / In Norwegian only at this time. The guidelines have 9 paragraphs stating the purpose of the school library, how it should function within the school, what sort of materials it is recommended to have in the collection. The text is only in Norwegian, but will be translated after a revision of the Public Library Act, fall 1996 - spring 1997. The revision has to be acknowledged by the Parliament. A paragraph concerning cooperation between the school and the public library is among those paragraphs that will have some changes.

3. Lois, décrets et règlements en matière de bibliothèques et de centres documentaires scolaires
Laws, Decrees and Rules about School Libraries and Resource Centers

362. Norges Offentlige Utredninger. Bibliotek i Norge. For kunnskap, kultur og Informasjon. (Libraries in Norway. For knowledge, culture and information). Oslo : Statens Forvaltning-stjeneste, 1991. 234 p.
Note: (NOU 1991: 14) (Note: contains a paragraph about school libraries).

363. Norway. Education Act no. 24 of the 13th of June 1969. § 10.2. (revised 1985).
Note: Norwegian: Lov av 13. juni 1969 nr. 24 om Grunnskolen § 10, nytt 2. ledd.
§10.2 states that the school shall have a library and a member of the staff who is responsible for library services. The school shall have both an educational and a general cultural function and must have an established cooperation with the public library in the municipality.

364. ___. Library Act. 1985 [20 December 1985; 108].
Note: With the new Library Act of 1985 the responsibility for the school libraries was transferred to the Education Act. (...) Section 6: Cooperation with schools. Section 10: Advisory services, etc.".

365. ___. Proposal of the culture department to a national Library Law. Culture Department, 1995.
Note: "To meet the pupils need of material for the education and to promote their interest for reading and literature there shall in the comprehensive school and in the upper secondary school be adequate divided school libraries".

366. ___. The Public Library Act. Act No. 108 of the 20th December 1985.
Note: Including latest admendments as of 11th June 1993. § 6: Co-operation with schools, § 10: Advisory services,etc.
Norwegian: Løv om folkebibliotek. Lov av 20 des. 1985 nr. 108.
Text available in English. This Act will be revised fall 1996 - spring 1997.

367. ___. The act concernig secondary education: Act of the 21th of June 1974. §12.
Note: Norwegian: Lov om videregående opplæring. Lov av 21 juni nr. 55. 1974, § 12.
§12 states that the school shall have a library service.
The revision of the Public Library Act (see note above) will influence on these paragraphs.

4. Situation des bibliothèques scolaires et des centres documentaires scolaires
Situation of School Libraries and Resource Centers

368. Horn, Ann. School libraries of Norway - a vital part of the national library network?. (paper given at the Open session of the Section of School Libraries, 53rd IFLA General Conference, Brighton, 1987).

Norvège (suite) / Norway (continued)

5. Rapports et autres documents / Reports and Other Documents

369. Kjekstad, Torny. *Library services for young adults : Norwegian cooperation projects between public and school libraries.* 8 p. (paper given at the Workshop "Library services for young adults", 60th IFLA Conference, La Habana, Cuba, August 21-27, 1994).

370. Nilsen, Sissel. "School Libraries in Norway: encouraging independant learning." *Scandinavian public quarterly* , vol. 29, no. 1, 1996, pp. 15-17.
Note: (based on a paper presented at the first National School Library Seminar, Bibliotecas Mediatecas Centros de Recursos, Lisboa, January 4-5, 1996).

371. Oyna, Ellen. *Cooperation between public and school libraries in Norway.* (paper given at the 19th annual Conference of the International Association of School Librarianship, Dragonskolan, Umea, Sweden, July 8-12, 1990).

372. Ulvik, Synnøve. *Portåpneren. Formidling av skjønnlitteratur i skolebibliotek - hvorfor, hvem, hvordan? (The gateopener. The school library as an intermediary to literature - why, to whom, how ?).* Oslo : Norsk Kulturråd, 1995. 54 p.

Nouvelle-Zélande / New Zealand

4. Situation des bibliothèques scolaires et des centres documentaires scolaires
Situation of School Libraries and Resource Centers

373. Andrews, Gail. *The Maori dimension in New Zealand schools.* (paper given at the Open session of the Section of School Libraries, 54th IFLA Conference, Sydney, 1988). (10-SCHOOL-2-E)

5. Rapports et autres documents / Reports and Other Documents

374. Andrews, Gail and Janice Frater. *School/community libraries in New Zealand.* Wellington, N.Z. : National Library of New Zealand, New Zealand Department of Education, 1987. 87 p.

375. Gawith, Gwen. "Teacher-librarianship: New Zealand's quantum leap." *International review of children's literature and librarianship* , vol. 5, no. 2, 1990, pp. 22-32.

Papouasie-Nouvelle-Guinée / Papua New Guinea

4. Situation des bibliothèques scolaires et des centres documentaires scolaires
Situation of School Libraries and Resource Centers

376. Paraide, Daniel. *School libraries in Papua New Guinea.* 12 p. (paper given at the IFLA Pre-session seminar on School Librarianship : Issues for Developing Countries, Caldes de Montbui, Spain, August 15-20, 1993).

5. Rapports et autres documents / Reports and Other Documents

377. Evans, John, and Ismael Isikel. "Improving the status of teacher-librarians in Papua New Guinea." *Education libraries journal* , vol. 36, no. 2, 1993, pp. 1-14.

378. Temu, Deveni. *Extending school library and community information services to a scatered population: Papua New Guinea,* (paper given at the Open session of the Section of School libraries, 46th IFLA General Conference, Manilla, 1980). (60/SCHO/2E)

Pérou / Peru

2. Politiques, normes et lignes directrices en bibliothéconomie scolaire
Policies, Standards and Guidelines in School Librarianship

379. Peru. *Normas para bibliotecas escolares.* Lima: 1984.
Note: Enquête menée en 1994 par Galler (1996).

5. Rapports et autres documents / Reports and Other Documents

380. Aliaga, Cesar. *The school library system : present situation and perspectives in Peru .* (paper
given at the 9th annual Conference of the International Association of School librarianship,
Ciudad Guayana, Venezuela, July 14-17, 1980).

Portugal

2. Politiques, normes et lignes directrices en bibliothéconomie scolaire
Policies, Standards and Guidelines in School Librarianship

381. Portugal. Ministerio da Educacao. Direccao dos Ensinos Basico e Secundario (DGEBS).
Tecnicas de documentacao. Lisboa : DGEBS, 1994. 4 v.
Note de Ramon Salaberria: Documentation pour aider les professeurs, qui est le fruit de la
collaboration entre bibliothécaires et professeurs. Comprend des définitions relatives aux
bibliothèque, aux médiathèques et aux centres de ressources scolaires et explique le traitement
technique de tous les types de documents.

3. Lois, décrets et règlements en matière de bibliothèques et de centres
documentaires scolaires
Laws, Decrees and Rules about School Libraries and Resource Centers

382. Portugal. *Ley 19-A/87 de 3 de Junho sobre Medidas de Emergencia sobre o ensino-*
aprendizagem da Lingua Portuguesa (Loi 19-A/87 du 3 de Juin sur les Mesures d'Urgence
pour l'enseignement-apprentissage de la Langue Portuguaise).
Note de Ramon Salaberria: L'article 4 dit: "Des bibliothèques seront créées dans tous les
établissements d'enseignement qui n'en n'ont pas encore; on prendra de mesures pour assurer
l'actualisation et l'enrichissement des collections des bibliothèques scolaires.".

5. Rapports et autres documents / Reports and Other Documents

383. Portugal. *Mediatecas escolares: genese e desenvolvimento de uma inovacao.* Lisboa : Instituto
de Inovacao Educacional, 1994.
Note de Ramon Salaberria: Bilan d'un programme pour la création de médiathèques scolaires avec
l'aide du fonds monétaire de l'Union Européenne et l'appui du Ministère de l'éducation.

Quatar

2. Politiques, normes et lignes directrices en bibliothéconomie scolaire
Policies, Standards and Guidelines in School Librarianship

384. Quatar. Ministry of Education. *Role of School libraries.* 74 p.
Note: Document in Arabic. Enquête menée en 1994 par Galler (1996).

Republique d'Irlande / Republic of Ireland

2. Politiques, normes et lignes directrices en bibliothéconomie scolaire
Policies, Standards and Guidelines in School Librarianship

385. Library Association of Ireland. *School Libraries : Guidelines for good practice.* Dublin: 1994.
     Enquête menée en 1994 par Galler (1996).

~~~~~~

Royaume-Uni / United Kingdom

1. Politiques générales d'éducation / General Educational Policies

386. Great Britain. Department for Education. *National Curriculum documents for England and Wales.* London : HMSO, 1995.

387. Great Britain. National Council for Educational Technology. *Libraries of the future : a pilot study of the impact of multimedia and communications technologies in libraries in education. Stage 1.* Coventry, G.B. : The Council, 1995. 46 p.

388. Great Britain. Office for Standards in Education. *Guidance on the inspection of nursery and primary schools.* London : HMSO, 1995. 130 p.

389. ___. *Guidance on the inspection of secondary schools.* London : HMSO, 1995. 138 p.

390. ___. *Guidance on the inspection of special schools.* London : HMSO, 1995. 136 p.

391. Scotland. Scottish Office. Education Department. *Curriculum and assessment in Scotland: National guidelines. (The five to fourteen curriculum - documents on sixteen subjects.).* Edinburgh, Scotland : The Office, 1991. onwards.

392. ___. *The Structure and balance of the five to fourteen curriculum.* Edinburgh, Scotland : The Office, 1993.

2. Politiques, normes et lignes directrices en bibliothéconomie scolaire
Policies, Standards and Guidelines in School Librarianship

393. Great Britain. Department of education and science. *Better libraries : good practice in schools.* London : The Department, 1989. 35 p.

394. Great Britain. Department of National Heritage. *Schools library services and financial delegation to schools.* London : HMSO, 1995. (Library and information series; no 21).

395. ___. *Investing in children : the future of library services for children and young people.* London : HMSO, 1995. (Library and Information series; no 22).

396. Great Britain. National Council for Educational Technology. *Information skills in the National Curriculum : Primary.* Coventry, G.B. : The Council, 1996. 20 p.

397. ___. *Information skills in the National Curriculum : Secondary.* Coventry, G.B. : The Council, 1996. 20 p.

398. Kinnell, Margaret. "Policy for secondary school library provision in England and Wales: an historical perspective." , vol. 27, no. 1, March 1995, pp. 17-26.

399. Library Association. *Learning resources in schools: Library Association guidelines for school libraries,* Ed. by Margaret Kinnell, London : The Association, 1992. 81 p.

Royaume-Uni (suite) / United Kingdom (continued)

2. Politiques, normes et lignes directrices en bibliothéconomie scolaire (suite)
Policies, Standards and Guidelines in School Librarianship (continued)

400. ___. *National curriculum and learning skills : curriculum guidance.* London : The Association, 1991.

401. ___. *Managing library resources in schools,* Ed. by Margaret Kinnell. London : The Association, 1994.

402. ___. *Curriculum Guidance : National Curriculum and effective learning.* London : The Association, 1996. 16 p.

403. Morrison, Marlene. "Policy frameworks for primary school libraries educational 'grey areas' in prospect and retrospect." *Education libraries journal*, vol. 35, no. 3, 1992, pp. 5-30.

404. Northern Ireland. Library and Information Services Council. *Libraries in primary schools : guidelines for good practice.* Ballymena, Ireland : The Council, 1995.

405. ___. *Libraries in post primary schools : guidelines for good practice.* Ballymena, Ireland : The Council, 1995.

406. School Library Association. *School libraries : steps in the right direction. Guidelines for a school library resource centre.* Swindon : SLA, 1989. 18 p.

407. ___. *SLA Guidelines.* Swindon : SLA.
   - *Designing and planning a primary school library,* 1994, 20 p.
   - *Designing and planning a secondary school library resource centre,* 1992, 20 p.
   - *Development planning for the school library resource centre,* 1993.
   - *Establishing a primary school library policy,* 1992, 8 p.
   - *Establishing a secondary school library policy,* 1996.
   - *Introducing new technology into the school library resource centre,* 1995, 24 p.
   - *Issue systems for the school library,* 1991, 6 p.
   - *Managing materials: basic routines in the school library,* 1992, 18 p.
   - *Matters of choice: selecting books for the library,* 1992, 26 p.
   - *Organizing voluntary help in the school library,* 1996, 20 p.
   - *The school library: annual report and statistics,* 1990, 6 p.
   - *The school library: preparing for inspection,* 1994, 20 p.
   - *Supporting specials needs in the secondary school library,* 1996.

4. Situation des bibliothèques scolaires et des centres documentaires scolaires
Situation of School Libraries and Resource Centers

408. Creaser, C. *A survey of library services to schools and children in the United Kingdom 1995-96.* Loughborough, G.B. : Loughborough University, 1996.

409. Great Britain. Department of Education and Science. *Library provision and use in 42 primary schools.* London : The Department, 1991.

410. ___. *A survey of secondary school libraries in six local education authorities : September 1988 - July 1989.* London : The Department, 1990. 12 p.

411. Great Britain. National Foundation for Educational Research. *Libraries of the future : an external evaluation : a proposal.* London : The Foundation, 1995. 11 p.

412. Streatfield, David, and Rob Davies. *The Library Power survey report on libraries and young people.* London : Library Association, 1995. 32 p. (British Library Research and Development Report no. 6217)

413. Wales. Library and Information Services Council. *The report of a working group on libraries in maintained secondary schools in Wales.* Cardiff, Wales : The Council, 1990. 11 p.

Royaume-Uni (suite) / United Kingdom (continued)

5. *Rapports et autres documents / Reports and Other Documents*

414. Baird, Nicola. *Setting up and running a school library.* London : Volunteer Service Overseas – Evaluating and Communicating our Overseas Experience, 1994. 137 p.

415. Book Trust. *Books in Schools Report 3.,* London : Book Trust, 1996. 32 p. (British National Bibliography Research Fund, Report 79.)

416. Elkin, J. "Formation des bibliothécaires des écoles secondaires en Angleterre et au Pays de Galles." *Documentaliste-sciences de l'information* ,vol. 27, no. 4-5, 1990, pp. 230-232.

417. Great Britain. National Council for Educational Technology. *The future curriculum with IT.* *Seminar Report.* Coventry, G.B. : The Council, 1993.

418. Heeks, Peggy, and Margaret Kinnell. *Managing change for school library services.* London : British Library Research and Development Department, 1992. (LIR report no. 89).

419. ___. *School libraries at work.* London : British Library Research and Development Department,1994. (LIR report no. 96).

420. Kinnell, Margaret. "Supporting the National Curriculum: English secondary school libraries during a period of transition." *The International information and library review* , vol. 26, no. 4, December 1994, pp. 257-270.

421. Streatfield, David, and Sharon Markless. *Invisible learning? The contribution of school libraries to teaching and learning. Report on the effective school library research project.* , London : British Library Research and Development Department,1994. 211 p. (LIR Report no. 98).

Russie / Russia

2. *Politiques, normes et lignes directrices en bibliothéconomie scolaire* *Policies, Standards and Guidelines in School Librarianship*

422. USSR. State Education Committee. *Tiopovoe (vremennoe) polozenie o bibliotheke obsheobrasovateljno shkoly.* 1991. 6 p.
Note: Enquête menée en 1994 par Galler (1996).

423. USSR. State Education Committee. *Technologia raboty shkolnoi bibliotheki: Intstructive-methodic materials and registration forms.* 1993. 74 p.
Note: Enquête menée en 1994 par Galler (1996).

Sénégal / Senegal

4. *Situation des bibliothèques scolaires et des centres documentaires scolaires* *Situation of School Libraries and Resource Centers*

424. Corréa, Antoinette Fall. *Les programmes de bibliothèques en milieu scolaire.* 47 p. (paper given at the IFLA Pre-session seminar on School Librarianship : Issues for Developing Countries, Caldes de Montbui, Spain, August 15-20, 1993).

Sénégal (suite) / Senegal (continued)

5. Rapports et autres documents / Reports and Other Documents

425. Corréa, Antoinette Fall. "La faim de lire des enfants du Sénégal." In: *Actes du Séminaire international sur la création de modèles de jumelages institutionnels à l'intention des bibliothèques du Sud et du Nord, Ottawa, 20-21 juin 1991.* Ottawa : Banque internationale d'information sur les états francophones, 1991, pp. 65-75.

Sierra Leone

5. Rapports et autres documents / Reports and Other Documents

426. Dillsworth, Gloria. "Sierra Leone Library Board." In: *Actes du Séminaire international sur la création de modèles de jumelages institutionnels à l'intention des bibliothèques du Sud et du Nord, Ottawa, 20-21 juin 1991.* Ottawa : Banque internationale d'information sur les états francophones, 1991, pp. 19-29.
Version en français: *Conseil des bibliothèques de la Sierra Leone.* 20 p.

Singapour / Singapore

2. Politiques, normes et lignes directrices en bibliothéconomie scolaire
Policies, Standards and Guidelines in School Librarianship

427. Library 2000 Review Committee. *Library 2000: investing in a learning nation.* Singapore: 1994. 171 p.

Suède / Sweden

2. Politiques, normes et lignes directrices en bibliothéconomie scolaire
Policies, Standards and Guidelines in School Librarianship

428. *Guidelines for the comprehensive school.* 1 p. Government bill 1992/1993.

429. *The Swedish language and literature.* 1 p. Official report 1992. School for education.

3. Lois, décrets et règlements en matière de bibliothèques et de centres documentaires scolaires
Laws, Decrees and Rules about School Libraries and Resource Centers

430. Sweden. Ministry of Culture. *Library Law.* 1996:1595.

5. Rapports et autres documents / Reports and Other Documents

431. Sweden. The Committee for Pedagogic Plans. *Plans for the Comprehensive School: the ending official report.* Stockholm: Allmänna förl., 1993. 138 p. (Official reports of the State, 1993:2).

432. ___. *School for education: primary report.* By the Committee for Pedagogic Plans. Stockholm: Allmänna förl., 1992. 469 p. (Official reports of the State, 1992:94).

Suède (suite) / Sweden (continued)

5. *Rapports et autres documents (suite) / Reports and Other Documents (continued)*

433. Swedish Library Association. Children and Young Adults Committee. *Putting the case for children's libraries. 5 arguments for children's library services.* Stockholm : Sveriges Allmanna Biblioteksforening, s.d. 4 p.
Version française:
Manifeste sur les bibliothèques pour enfants: 5 arguments, élaborés par la Commission pour enfants et jeunes de l'Association générale des Bibliothèques de Suède, en faveur des bibliothèques pour enfants, 4 p.

Suisse / Switzerland

2. *Politiques, normes et lignes directrices en bibliothéconomie scolaire*
Policies, Standards and Guidelines in School Librarianship

434. *Richtlinien for Schulbibliotheken. (Guidelines for School Libraries). Grundsätze, technische Daten und praktische Beispiele für die Gründung, des Ausbau und die Führung allgemeiner öffentlichen Bibliotheken.* Bern: Schweizer Bibliotheksdienst, 1990.
Note: Enquête menée en 1994 par Galler (1996).

4. *Situation des bibliothèques scolaires et des centres documentaires scolaires*
Situation of School Libraries and Resource Centers

435. Duparc, Madeleine. "Les bibliothèques et centres de documentation suisses et genevois." *Inter-CDI*, no. 118, juillet-août 1992, pp. 51-55.

Swaziland

4. *Situation des bibliothèques scolaires et des centres documentaires scolaires*
Situation of School Libraries and Resource Centers

436. Tawete, Felix K. *The state of school libraries in Swaziland.* 12 p. (paper given at the IFLA Pre-session seminar on School Librarianship : Issues for Developing Countries, Caldes de Montbui, Spain, August 15-20, 1993).

5. *Rapports et autres documents / Reports and Other Documents*

437. Fakudze, Nomcebo Queeneth. *The role of libraries in schools in Swaziland. A study of the 1990s and implications for the twenty-first century. A dissertation submitted in partial fulfilment of the degree of B.A.* Leeds, Swaziland : Metropolitan University, 1993.

438. Kingsley, Ben. "The story of Swaziland National Library Service. Its achievements to date and plans for the future." In: *Libraries in Swaziland Library Association Conference and Annual General Meeting, Kwaluseni, Swaziland, June 21st, 1991.*

439. Mabuza, Sakhepi Regina. *An investigation of the effective use of school libraries in high schools in Swaziland,* A dissertation submitted in partial fulfilment of the requirements for the degree of Bachelor of Education. Kwaluseni, Swaziland : University of Swaziland, 1992.

Thaïlande / Thailand

2. *Politiques, normes et lignes directrices en bibliothéconomie scolaire*
Policies, Standards and Guidelines in School Librarianship

440. Thai Library Association. *Library Standards.* Bangkok, 1994. 75 p. Under the patronage of HRH Princess Mahachaki Sirindhorn.,
Note: Enquête menée en 1994 par Galler (1996).

Trinidad et Tobago

1. *Politiques générales d'éducation / General Educational Policies*

441. Trinidad and Tobago. Ministry of Education. *Policy Paper (1993-2000).* A white paper produced by The National Task Force on Education, 1993, p. 34-37.
Note: Enquête menée en 1994 par Galler (1996).

2. *Politiques, normes et lignes directrices en bibliothéconomie scolaire*
Policies, Standards and Guidelines in School Librarianship

442. Trinidad and Tobago. Ministry of Education. *Solving the Research Mystery: The BIG SIX Information Problem Solving Process; An eight part course developed by the School Libraries Division in collaboration with the Schools Broadcasting Unit; Teacher's Handbook.* S.l. : 1996.

Tunisie / Tunisia

4. *Situation des bibliothèques scolaires et des centres documentaires scolaires*
Situation of School Libraries and Resource Centers

443. Fettahi, Ali. *Les bibliothèques scolaires en Tunisie.* 10 p. (paper given at the IFLA Pre-session seminar on School Librarianship : Issues for Developing Countries, Caldes de Montbui, Spain, August 15-20, 1993).

Turquie / Turkey

4. *Situation des bibliothèques scolaires et des centres documentaires scolaires*
Situation of School Libraries and Resource Centers

444. Önal, Inci. *The future roles and functions of the school libraries : a project for Turkish school libraries,* 7 p. In: Booklet 3: Library serving the general public, pp. 78-81. (paper given the Open session of the Section of School Libraries, 61st IFLA Conference, Istanbul, Turkey, August 20-26, 1995). (009-SCHOOL-1-E).

445. ___. "School library development in Turkey." *Türk kütüphaneciligi* ,vol. 9, no. 3, 1995, pp. 255-257.

446. Turkiye Cumhuriyeti. Milli Egitim Bakanligi. *Okul Kütüphaneleri Yönetmeligi (Guidelines for School Libraries).* Ankara : Mili Egitim Basimevi, 1990. 18 p.
Note: Enquête menée en 1994 par Galler (1996).

Venezuela

4. Situation des bibliothèques scolaires et des centres documentaires scolaires
Situation of School Libraries and Resource Centers

447. Penna, Carlos Victor. "The national system of library and information services of Venezuela."
Journal of library history, vol. 17, no. 2, 1982, pp. 117-143.

Zimbabwe

4. Situation des bibliothèques scolaires et des centres documentaires scolaires
Situation of School Libraries and Resource Centers

448. Stringer, Roger. *Report on the compilation and publication of the Directory of Zimbabwe
Publishers.* 4 p. (paper given at the IFLA Pre-session seminar on School Librarianship :
Issues for Developing Countries, Caldes de Montbui, Spain, August 15-20, 1993).

Répertoires et listes bibliographiques / Directories and bibliographies

449. Banque internationale d'information sur les états francophones. *Profils géodocumentaires des
états et gouvernements membres des sommets francophones.* Éd. mise à jour, Ottawa :
BIEF, mars 1993. 1 classeur, pag. multiple.

450. "Bibliographie sélective = selective bibliography." In: *Actes du Séminaire international sur la
création de modèles de jumelages institutionnels à l'intention des bibliothèques du Sud et
du Nord, Ottawa, 20-21 juin 1991.* Ottawa : Banque internationale d'information sur les
états francophones, 1991, pp. 141-152.

451. Brown, Gerald R. "Resources for school library development." *School libraries worldwide*,
vol. 1, no. 2, 1995, pp. 30-76.

452. Oberg, Dianne, and Kaye Steward. *Connections. School library Associations and contact
people worldwide.* Kalamazoo, MI : International Association of School Librarianship, 1994.
96 p.

453. *School libraries : a reading list.* Compiled by Peggy Heeks. London : The Library Association,
1995. 9 p.

454. Watt, Michael G. "Information services in an age of education reform : a review of developments
in four countries." *School library media quarterly*, vol. 23, no. 2, Winter 1995, pp. 115-122.
Note: Developments of the Educational Resources Information Center (ERIC), British Education Index
(BEI), Canadian Education Index (CEI) and Australian Education Index (AEI).

455. ___. "Systems for exchanging information on instructional resources : a review of recent
services in four countries." *School media library quarterly*, vol. 23, no. 4, Summer 1995, pp.
239-247.
Note: Developments of the National Information Center for Educational Media (NICEM, U.S.),
Educational Products Information Exchange (EPIE) Institute (U.S.), Ontario Institute for Studies in
Education (OISE, Canada), NERIS Trust (UK), and Curriculum Corporation (Australia).

~~~~~~

A
Abdel-Motey, Yaser 12
Adcock, Donald C. 27
Aguiar, Mercedes 180
Alberta Education 133, 134
Ali, Muhaimad S.S 322
Aliaga, Cesar 380
Amalia, Suzana 179
American Association of School Librarians 209, 210, 211
Amundsen, Esme 87
Association for Educational Communications and Technology 211
American Library Association 212
Amey, J. Larry (Ed.) 28, 29
Anderson, Beatrice L. 308
Andresen, Åse Foss 358
Andrews, Gail 373, 374
Argentina 72,73, 74, 76
Argentina. Buenos Aires (Provincia). Dirección General de 73
Argentina. Dirección Nacional de Investigación. Experiment 74
Argentina. Tierra del Fuego: Dirección de Bibliotecas Esco 76
Asean Committee on Culture and Information 292
Association belge de Documentation (Ed.) 109
Association for Teacher-Librarianship in Canada 127
Australian Education Council 79
Australian Library and Information Association 80, 81, 91
Australian School Library Association 81, 91

B
Baffour-Awuah, Margaret 113, 116
Bahnisch, Brian (Dir.) 87
Baird, Nicola 414
Banque internationale d'information sur les états francophones 449
Baro, Mónica 205, 206
Bawa, Rookaya 68
Bayard-Pierlot, Jacqueline 254
Beaulac, Jacqueline 148
Benneto, Liz 82
Bernhard, Paulette 2, 13, 14, 30, 31, 32, 33, 34, 35, 36, 148
Birglin, Marie-José 254
Bodart, Jacques108
Book Trust 415
Botswana 111
Boyce, Emily S. 215
Brasil 117
Breithaupt, Renate 70
Breton, Lise 35, 36
British Columbia. Ministry of Education 123, 135, 136
British Columbia Teacher–Librarians' Association 136
Brown, Gerald R. 451
Butlen, Max 255
Butler, R. 228

C
Callison, Daniel 231
Canadian School Library Association 128, 129, 130
Canarias 198

4.2

INDEX DES TITRES   -   INDEX OF TITLES

~~~~~~

4.2

INDEX DES PAYS   -   INDEX OF COUNTRIES

Index en français
~~~~~~~~~~~~~~~~~~~~~~~~~

~~~~~~

128

Index in English

Cinquième partie / Part Five

𝑥 𝑥 𝑥 𝑥 𝑥

Ressources sur les habiletés d'information et sur les technologies de l'information en éducation

~~~

Resources about Information Skills and Information Technology in Education

~~~

Par / By : Paulette Bernhard

5.1 Développer les habiletés d'information en relation avec les programmes d'études du primaire et du secondaire : un choix de ressources (1988-1997)

Developing Information Skills through Primary and Secondary Education Curricula : a Selection of Resources (1988-1997)

5.2 Les technologies de l'information et de la communication (TIC) en éducation : une sélection de ressources à l'intention des responsables de bibliothèques et de centres documentaires scolaires

Information Technologies (IT) in Education : a Selection of Resources for Those Responsible for School Libraries and Resources Centers

5.1

DÉVELOPPER LES HABILETÉS D'INFORMATION EN RELATION AVEC LES PROGRAMMES D'ÉTUDES DU PRIMAIRE ET DU SECONDAIRE : UN CHOIX DE RESSOURCES (1988-1997)

DEVELOPING INFORMATION SKILLS THROUGH PRIMARY AND SECONDARY EDUCATION CURRICULA : A SELECTION OF RESOURCES (1988-1997)

Par / By Paulette Bernhard

» INTRODUCTION

On trouvera dans les pages qui suivent la mention d'environ quatre-vingts ressources autant impri-mées qu'en ligne, quelquefois les deux. Elles traitent des différentes facettes de la «culture de l'infor-mation» et de la formation dans ce domaine, en relation avec les programmes d'études des enseigne-ments primaire et secondaire. On y trouvera aussi une section sur le partenariat entre bibliothécaires/ spécialistes de l'information et enseignants pour la planification d'activités conjointes. Dans chaque catégorie, les ressources en français précèdent celles en anglais. Tous les sites accessibles en ligne ont été vérifiés le 29 mai 1997.

In the following pages, you will find about eighty references of resources in print, on line or, sometimes, both. They all deal with the different facets of "information literacy" and instruction in this area, in relation to the curriculum in primary and secondary education. A final section is devoted to showing how school librarians/teacher-librarians and teachers can plan units cooperatively. In each category, resources in French precede the ones in English. All Web sites have been checked on May, 29, 1997.

» DÉFINITION DU CONCEPT DE MAÎTRISE DE L'INFORMATION
DEFINING THE CONCEPT OF INFORMATION LITERACY

Behrens, Shirley L. "A conceptual analysis and historical overview odf information literacy." *College and research libraries,* vol. 55, no 4, 1994, pp. 309-322.

Breivik, Patricia Senn; Gee, Elwood Gordon. *Information literacy : revolution in the library.* New York; London: American Council on Education; Collier Macmillan, 1989. xi-250 p. (American Council on Education/ Macmillan series on higher education)

Carefoot, Lilian. "Information skills: what does it mean to be information literate ? *School libraries in Canada,* vol. 14, no2, 1994, pp. 11-15.

Eisenberg, Michael B.; Johnson, Doug. *Computer skills for information problem-solving: learning and teaching technology in context.* Syracuse, NY: ERIC Clearinghouse on information technology, March 1996. (ERIC Digest EDO-IR-96-04) (Also on line) URL address: http://ericir.syr.edu/ithome/digests/computerskills.html

McLure, Charles R. "Network literacy: a role for the librarian?." *Information technology and libraries,* vol. 13, no 2, 1994, pp. 115-125.

Shapiro, Jeremy J.; Hughes, Shelley K. "Information literacy as a liberal art." *Educom review*, vol.31, no 2, March/April 1996. (On line) URL address:
http://www.educom.edu/web/pubs/review/reviewArticles/31231.html

» DÉVELOPPER LA FORMATION À LA MAÎTRISE DE L'INFORMATION AU PRIMAIRE ET AU SECONDAIRE
DEVELOPING INFORMATION LITERACY INSTRUCTION IN PRIMARY AND SECONDARY EDUCATION

Ressources en français

Alava, Séraphin. "Éléments pour une didactique de la médiation documentaire." *Documentaliste-Sciences de l'information*, vol. 30, no 1, 1993, pp. 14-18.

Alava, S. "Mémoires, médias et apprentissages: l'enseignant documentaliste au coeur d'une autre stratégie d'enseignement." *Cahiers de la Documentation*, no 1, 1996, pp. 14-27.

Alberta Education. Language Services Branch. *Enseignement et recherche: guide pour le développement des habiletés de recherche*. Edmonton : Alberta Education, 1991. 87 p.

Association for Teacher-Librarianship in Canada. *Charte des droits de l'élève à l'ère de l'information*. Traduction par Paulette Bernhard. Vancouver: ATLC, 1995. 1 p.
(Aussi en ligne) Adresse URL: http://tornade.ERE.UMontreal.CA/~bernh/secondai/educat/charte.htm

Bernhard, Paulette. "Des habiletés d'information à la maîtrise de l'information." In: *Comment informatiser l'école?* Coordonné par Gérard Puimatto et Robert Bibeau. Montréal: Les Publications du Québec; Paris: Centre national de documentation pédagogique, 1997, pp. 151-162. (La collection de l'ingénierie éducative)

Cégep de Sainte-Foy. Guide méthodologique pour vos recherches (Québec) (En ligne) Adresse URL: http://www.aide-doc.qc.ca/voilier/HtmlVoilier/RechDocDepart.html

Chevalier, Brigitte; Colin, Michelle. *Exploiter l'information au CDI*. Paris: Institut national de recherche pédagogique, 1991. 106 P. (Rencontres pédagogiques; 29)

"Continuités et ruptures : bibliothèques et centres documentaires de la maternelle à l'université". *Argos: revue des BCD et des CDI*, no 14, mars 1995, 88 p. [numéro thématique]

Former et apprendre à s'informer : pour une culture de l'information. Paris: ADBS Éditions, 1993. 18 + 110 p.

France. Ministère de l'Éducation nationale. Direction des lycées et collèges. *Pour une pédagogie documentaire. Expériences de recherche au collège*. Paris: le ministère, sd. 219 p.

Guertin, Hélène. *CHERCHER POUR TROUVER ! Site dédié aux élèves et aux éducateurs des écoles secondaires*. (site créé en1996) (En ligne). Adresse URL:
http://tornade.ERE.UMontreal.CA/~bernh/secondai/index.html

Laliberté-Lefebvre, Claire. "Le travail intellectuel en bibliothèque et le développement des structures mentales des étudiants du collégial." *Argus*, vol. 25, no 1, 1996, pp. 29-39.

Léveillé, Yves. *Les 6 étapes d'un projet de recherche. Détail d'une démarche complète de recherche d'information*. (En ligne). Adresse URL:
http://tornade.ere.umontreal.ca/~guertinh/secondai/projet/index.htm

Marquis, Luce. *Apprendre à s'informer: projets d'animation*. 2e éd. revue et augmentée. Montréal : Les Éditions ASTED, 1996. 195 p. (Clé en main)

Resources in English

Alberta Education. Curriculum Support Branch. *Focus on research: a guide to developing students' research skills.* Edmonton : Alberta Education, 1990. 86 p.

Atkinson, J.; Scott, N. "Rethinking information skills teaching." *Learning resources journal,* vol. 11, no 2, 1995, pp. 45-48.

Association for Teacher-Librarianship in Canada. *Students'bill of information rights.* Vancouver: ATLC, 1995. 1 p.

Australian School Library Association. *Teaching information skills.* Perth: ASLA, 1997. (CD-ROM)

Baldwin, Shart. "Taking the reading out of research." *School libraries in Canada,* vol. 16, no 4, 1996, pp. 18-20.

Best, R.; Abbott, F.; Taylor, M. *Teaching skills for learning: information skills in initial teacher education.* London: British Library, 1990. (Library and information research report; 78).

Bleakley, Ann; Carrigan, Jackie L. *Resource–based learning activities. Information literacy for high school students.* Chicago, IL : American Library Association, 1994. 227 p.

British Columbia. Ministry of Education. *Developing independant learners. The role of the school library resource centre.* Victoria: The ministry, 1991. 101 p.

Colorado. State Library and Adult Education Office. *Information literacy guidelines.* Denver, CO: State Library and Adult Education Office, Colorado Department of Education, Colorado Educational Media Association, 1994.

Colorado. State Library and Adult Education Office. *Model information literacy standards.* Denver, CO: State Library and Adult Education Office, Colorado Department of Education, 1994.

Corcoran, Fran; Langlois, Dianne. "Instruction in the use of library media centers in schools." In: American Library Association. Library Instruction Round Table. *The LIRT Library Instruction Handbook.* Edited by May Brottman and Mary Loe. Englewook, Colorado: Libraries Unlimited, 1990, pp. 77-89.

Cowley, J. *Post-induction information skills teaching in UK higher education: six studies.* London: British Library, 1990. (British Library Research Paper; 76).

Curriculum and Lesson Plans for Information Literacy. (On line) URL address: http://www.sos.net/home/wlma/curplan.htm

Eisenberg, Michael B.; Berkowitz, Robert E. *Information problem-solving : The big six skills approach to library and information skills instruction.* Norwood, NJ: Ablex Publishing, 1990.

Eisenberg, Michael B.; Berkowitz, Robert E. *Helping with homework: a parent's guide to information problem-solving.* Syracuse, N.Y.: ERIC Clearinghouse on Information & Technology, 1996. 182 p.

Eisenberg, Michael B.; Brown, Michael K. "Current themes regarding library and information skills Instruction : research supporting and research lacking." *School libray media quarterly,* vol. 20, no 2, 1992, pp.103-110.

Fasick, Adele M. "What research tells us about children's use of information media." *Canadian library journal,* vol. 49, no 1, 1992, pp. 51-54.

Garland, Kathleen. "The information serach process: a study of elements associated with meaningful research tasks." *School library media annual,* vol. 13, 1995, pp. 171-183.

Gawith, Gwen. *Power learning. A student's guide to success.* Auckland: Longman Paul Limited, 1991. 136 p.

Gawith, Gwen. *Ripping into Research. Information skills for secondary and tertiary students.* Auckland : Longman Paul Limited, 1991. 60 p.

Grover, Robert; Eisenberg, Michael. Information skills: the "Big Six Models. Castle Rock, CO: Hi Willow, 1993. (Video)

Hanani, Uri; Frank, Ariel. "Intelligent information harvesting architecture: an application to a high school environment." In : *Online Information 96. 20th international online information meeting.* Proceedings. London, 3-5 December 1996. Ed. by David I. Raitt and Ben Jeapes. Oxford : Learned Information Ltd, 1996, pp. 211-220.

Herring, James. *Teaching information skills in schools.* London: Library Association Publishing, 1996. 144 p.

Hodgson, E.A.; Quigley, Mary Liz. *On your own. A guide to competing independent study projects.* London : Oakridge Secondary School, 1994. 40 p.

Information Literacy Standards for Student Learning. Prepared by the AASL/AECT National Guidelines Vision Committee. Draft #5. October 7, 1996. (On line) URL address: http://www.ala.org/aasl/stndsdrft5.html

Irving, A.; Carter, C. *Wider horizons: online information services in schools.* London: British Library, 1990. (Library and information research report; report 80).

Irving, A.; Wilkinson, J.; Hubbard, G.; Marland, M. *Seminar on educating information users in schools.* London: British Library, 1990. (British Library Research Paper no 34).

Kuhlthau, Carol Collier. "Implementing a process approach to information skills: a study identifying indicators of success in library media programs." *School library media quarterly, vol. 22,* no 1, Fall 1993, pp. 11-18.

Kuhlthau, Carol Collier. "The process of learning from information". *School libraries worldwide,* vol. 1, no 1, 1995, pp. 1-12.

Kuhlthau, Carol Collier. *Seeking meaning : a process approach to library and information services.* Norwood, NJ : Ablex Pub. Corp., c1993. xxvi, 199 p. (Information management, policy, and services)

Kuhlthau, Carol C. *Teaching the library research process.* 2nd ed. Metuchen, N.J. : The Scarecrow Press, 1994. xv, 189 p.

"Learning from information." *School libraries worldwide,* vol. 1, no 1, 1995, 86 p. [numéro thématique]

Library Association. *Curriculum guidance: national curriculum and effective learning.* London: The Library Association, 1996. 16 p.

Linning, Lyn. "Metacognition and resource based learning." *Access,* vol. 5, no 3, 1991, p. 16-18.

McKenzie, Jamieson. *A measure of student success: assessing information problem solving skills.* (On line). URL address: http://fromnowon.org/oakharbor.html

Markless, S.; Streatfield, D. *Liaison officer for information skills in schools: report on the project.* London: British Library, 1990. (British Library R & D Report; 5995).

Media Literacy Online Project (University of Oregon). "Project concerned with helping students develop an informed and critical understanding of the nature of the mass media, the techniques used by them, and the impact of these techniques." (On line) URL address: http://interact.uoregon.edu/MediaLit/HomePage

Mendrinos, Roxanne. *Building information literacy using high technology : a guide for schools and libraries.* Englewood, Colo. : Libraries Unlimited, 1994. x-190 p.

Ochs, Mary, Coons, Bill; Van Ostrand, Darla; Barnes, Susan. *Assessing the value of an information literacy program.* Ithaca, NY.: Cornell University, Albert A. Mann Library. 1991. 105 p. (ERIC ED 340 385)

Pitts, Judy. "The 1993-94 AASL/Highsmith Research Award Study: mental models of information." Ed. by Joy H. McGregor and Barabra K. Stripling. School library media annual, vol. 13, 1995, pp. 187-200.

Rogers, Rick (Ed.) *Teaching information skills: a review of the research and its impact on education.* London: Bowker Saur, 1994. xii-101 p. (British Library Research Series)

Sanger, J. (Ed.) *The teaching, handling Infromation and learning project.* London: British Library, 1989. (Library and information research report; Report 67).

Schambler, Linda. "The role of libraries in literacy education." (ERIC digest). *Emergency librarian,* vol. 19, no 2, 1991, pp. 34-35.

Stripling, Barabra K.; Pitts, Judy. *Brainstorms and bkueprints: teaching library research as a thinking process.* Englewood, CO: Libraries Unlimited, 1988. xv-181 p.

Walster, Dian; Welborn, Lynda. "Student-centered information literacy programs: the Colorado vision." *School library media annual,* vol. 13, 1995, pp. 45-53.

Walster, Dian; Welborn, Lynda. "Alternative assessment for Colorado's information literacy guidelines: interin report on the 1994-95 AASL/Highsmith Research Award Project." *School library media annual,* vol. 13, 1995, pp. 206-214.

Washington Library Media Association Ad Hoc Committee on Essential Learnings. *Essential learnings and school libraries.* Sept. 1996. (On line) URL address: http://www.wlma.org/literacy/eslslibs.htm

Weisburg, Hilda K. "The information curriculum : teaching concepts for the virtual library environment." *School library media annual,* vol. 12, 1994, pp. 63-68.

» PLANIFICATION D'ACTIVITÉS CONJOINTES
COOPERATIVE PLANNING AND TEACHING

Ressources en français

Bernhard, Paulette (Ed.). *Bibliothécaires et enseignants: un partenariat prometteur. Document d'ac-compagnement. Recueil des projets...* Montréal: Corporation des bibliothécaires professionnels du Québec, mai 1996. 2 vol. 37 p. (PRIMAIRE) + 74 p. (SECONDAIRE) (Accompagne le vidéogramme du même titre réalisé par Paulette Bernhard et Patrick Delobel)

Bernhard, Paulette; Leclerc, Jocelyne (Collab.). "Le partenariat pour la planification d'activités conjointes: sources bibliographiques annotées." *Éducation et francophonie,* vol. XXIV, nos 1 et 2, 1996, pp. 112-119. Note: Aussi disponible sur le Web, adresse URL: http://www.acelf.ca/revue/articles/bernhard.html

Couturier, Marco. Ressources en Histoire du Canada et du Québec. Programme d'histoire 414, secondaire IV. (Site développé en 1997). (En ligne) Adresse URL: http://tornade.ERE.UMontreal.CA/~couturim/index414.html

Resources in English

Arany, Ruth Ann. "Canada: a cooperatively planned teaching unit." *Indiana media journal,* vol. 13, no 2, 1991, pp. 21-26.

Eisenberg, Michael B.; Berkowitz, Robert E. *Curriculum initiative : an agenda and strategy for library media programs.* Norwood, N.J.: Ablex Pub. Corp., c1988. xix-180 p.

Farmer, Lesley S. *Creative partnership: librarians and teachers working together.* Worthington, Ohio: Linworth, 1993.

Landcare Education (Australia). Information or projects that may be useful for landcare education at primary or secondary school level. (On line) URL address: http://www.agfor.unimelb.edu.au/LCweb/lclibrary/edulcare.html

Little, Tami J. Banana Splits for Big Six. (On line). URL address: http://ericir.syr.edu/big6/Action/Lessons/K-12/bansplit.html

Mendrinos, Roxanne. "Teacher-library media specialist partnership." In: *Building information literacy using high technology a guide for schools and libraries.* Englewood, Colo.: Libraries Unlimited, 1994, pp. 11-12.

The teacher-librarians of the Toronto Board of Education. The Role of the Teacher-Librarian to "share their vision of student learning with principals, teachers, students, parents, Board administrators and trustees". (On line). URL address: http://www.target.tbe.edu/lib/model/lib-inf/lib-inf2.html

Turner, Philip. "What help do teachers want, and what will they do to get it ?" *School library media quarterly,* vol. 24, no 4, 1996, pp. 208-212.

Washington Library Media Association Online. *Curriculum and lesson plans for information Literacy.* (On line). URL address: http://www.wlma.org/literacy/curplan.htm

Wolcott, Linda Lachance. "Understanding how teachers plan: stategies for successful instructional partnerships." *School library media quarterly,* vol. 22, no 3, 1994, pp. 161-165.

Winners: a collection of cooperatively developed teaching units for resource-based learning. Ed. by Linda Knight; assistant editor, Susan Leppington. Vancouver, B.C.: Association for Teacher-Librarianship in Canada, 1996. x-121 p.

1. Les animaux

ANIMALS - index 1996

Michèle Lévesque

5.2

LES TECHNOLOGIES DE L'INFORMATION ET DE LA COMMUNICATION (TIC) EN ÉDUCATION : UNE SÉLECTION DE RESSOURCES À L'INTENTION DES RESPONSABLES DE BIBLIOTHÈQUES ET DE CENTRES DOCUMENTAIRES SCOLAIRES

INFORMATION TECHNOLOGIES (IT) IN EDUCATION : A SELECTION OF RESOURCES FOR THOSE RESPONSIBLE FOR SCHOOL LIBRARIES AND RESOURCE CENTERS

Par / By Paulette Bernhard

PLAN   »   INTRODUCTION
         »   SOURCES GÉNÉRALES / GENERAL SOURCES
         »   EXPLOITATION DES RESSOURCES DE L'INTERNET EN ÉDUCATION
            USE OF INTERNET RESOURCES IN EDUCATION
         »   QUELQUES SITES EN ÉDUCATION / A GLANCE AT SOME SITES IN EDUCATION

» INTRODUCTION

On trouvera dans les pages qui suivent la mention d'une soixantaine de ressources parues depuis 1992 autant imprimées qu'en ligne, quelquefois les deux. Elles couvrent plusieurs types d'information électronique, depuis la base de données jusqu'aux ressources de l'internet, en passant par le CD-ROM. Nous présentons en premier lieu les ressources traitant de la problématique générale des technologies de l'information en éducation, suivies par une série de ressources portant plus spécifiquement sur l'exploitation des ressources de l'internet et, enfin, par une courte rubrique pointant sur quelques sites d'intérêt général développés en éducation en Australie, au Canada, en France et aux États-Unis. Dans chaque catégorie, les ressources en français précèdent celles en anglais. Tous les sites accessibles en ligne ont été vérifiés le 29 mai 1997.

In the following pages, you will find about sixty references of resources published since 1992 in print, on line or, sometimes, both. They cover several types of electronic information, from databases to CD-ROMs to Internet resources. First come the resources covering the general question of information technologies in education; second, a series of resources dealing more specifically with use of Internet resources; and finally, a short section pointing to some sites of general interest developed in education in Australia, Canada, France and the United States. In each category, resources in French precede the ones in English. All Web sites have been checked on May, 29, 1997.

» SOURCES GÉNÉRALES / GENERAL SOURCES

Ressources en français

Industrie Canada. Direction du développement des communications. *Les possibilités éducatives de l'autoroute de l'information au Canada : utilisation et instauration des technologies de l'information et communications en éducation.* Par Luc Fournier et Kim MacKinnon. Ottawa: octobre1994, viii, 102 p. + annexes.

"Internet dans le monde éducatif." *Les dossiers de l'ingénierie éducative,* no 24, déc. 1996. 64 p.

Morizio, Claude; Saj, Marie-Paule; Souchaud, Michel. *Les technologies de l'information au CDI.* Paris: Hachette Éduction, 1996. 190 p.

Québec, Conseil de la Science et de la Technologie. *Miser sur le savoir : rapport de conjoncture 1994.* Québec: Gouvernement du Québec, 1994. 3 vol. (1. La culture scientifique et technologique. 100 p. 2. Les nouvelles technologies de l'information. 120 p. 3. Les PME technologiques. 64 p.)

Québec. Conseil supérieur de l'Éducation. *Rapport annuel 1993-1994 sur l'état et les besoins de l'éducation : les nouvelles technologies de l'information et de la communication : des engagements pressants.* Sainte-Foy : Les Publications du Québec, 1994. 52 p.

138

Réginald Grégoire Inc.; Bracewell, Robert; Laferrière, Thérèse. *L'apport des nouvelles technologies de l'information et de la communication (NTIC) à l'apprentissage des élèves du primaire et du secondaire. Revue documentaire.* 1er août 1996. SCHOOLNET / RESCOL. (En ligne) Adresse URL: http://www.tact.fse.ulaval.ca/fr/html/apportnt.html

Tardif, Jacques. Une condition incontournable aux promesses des NTIC en apprentissage: une pédagogie rigoureuse. Cnférence d'ouverture du congrès de l'AQUOPS, 1996. (En ligne) Adresse URL: http://aquops.educ.infinit.net/ntic/tic_article_1.html

Resources in English

Berger, Pam; Kinnell, Susan. "CD-ROM and curriculum: the critical connection." *Information searcher*, vol. 6, no 4, 1994, pp. 1 + 7-10.

Casey, Jean M. *Early literacy: the empowerment of technology.* Englewood, CO: Libraries Unlimited, 1997. xxi-178 p.

Center for Applied Special Technology. The role of online communications in schools : a national study. (On line) URL address: http://www.cast.org/stsstudy.html

Clyde, Laurel A. "New technologies, information access and educational outcomes." *Emergency librarian*, vol. 19, no 3, 1992, pp. 8-18.

Great Britain. National Council for Educational Technology . *Highways for learning: an introduction to the Internet for schools and colleges.* (On line) URL address: http://www.ncet.org.uk/publications/highways/

Hay, Lyn; Henri, James (Eds.). *A meeting of the minds: ITEC virtual conference '96 proceedings.* (Perth): Australian School Library Association, 1996. 232 p.

Herring, James E. *Information technology in schools: the role of the school librarian and the teacher.* 2nd ed. of *The microcomputer, the school librarian and the teacher.* London, Library Association Publishing, 1992. x, 158 p.

ICONNECT. *Connecting learners to information.* Chicago: American Association of School Librarians. (ICONnect publication series) 1. How to connect to the Internet. 1996. 16 p. 2. Curriculum connection on the 'Net. 1996. 16 p.

The impact of technology. Annotated bibliography providing links to surveys, bibliographies, literature re-views, articles, reports, and case studies... (On line) URL address: http://www.mcrel.org/connect/tech/impact.html

Mendrinos, Roxanne Baxter. "CD-ROM and the school library media center." *Schol library media annual*, vol. 12, 1994, pp. 21-32.

Pappas, Marjorie. *Transforming library media centers with technology.* McHenry, IL: Follett Software Company, 1993. 112 p.

Réginald Grégoire Inc.; Bracewell, Robert; Laferrière, Thérèse. *The contribution of new technologies to learning and teachers in elementary ans secondary schools. Documentary review.* August 1st, 1996. SCHOOLNET / RESCOL. (On line) URL address: http://www.tact.fse.ulaval.ca/fr/html/impactnt.html

Rothenberg, Dianne. "Information technology in education." *Annual review of information science and technology*, vol. 29, 1994, pp. 277-302.

Simeone, Paula. Integrating information technology into educational curriculums. (On line) URL address: http://www.alia.org.au/publications/orana/33.1/simeone.html

Waters, David. "New technology and the image of the school library media center." *School library media quarterly*, vol. 22, no 4, 1994, pp. 213-220.

Wright, Kieth. *The challenge of technology: action strategies for the school library media specialist* Chicago: American Library Association, 1993. Env. 140 p.

» EXPLOITATION DES RESSOURCES DE L'INTERNET EN ÉDUCATION
USE OF INTERNET RESOURCES IN EDUCATION

Ressources en français

Alava, Séraphin. "Autoroutes de l'information et apprentissages documentaires." *Documentaliste-Sciences de l'information*, vol. 33, no 3, 1996, pp. 135-141.

Alava, Séraphin. "Naviguer sans se noyer: multimédia et médiation documentaire." *Inter-CDI*, no 132, nov.-déc. 1994, pp. 64-68. ET "Naviguer sans se noyer (suite). Du cabotage au grand large: la recherche documentaire sur hypermédia." *Inter-CDI*, no 137, sept.-oct. 1995, pp. 74-79.

Conférence des recteurs et des principaux des universités du Québec. Sous-comité des bibliothèques. *Guide d'initiation à la recherche sur Internet (GIRI)*. Par Line Cormier, Luc Grondin, Diane Poirier et Marc Waller. Montréal: CRÉPUQ, 1996. Note: aussi disponible sur le Web: URL: http://infopuq.uquebec.ca/~qc13251 -

Conférence des recteurs et des principaux des universités du Québec. Sous-comite des bibliothèques. *GIRI 2 - Guide des indispensables de la recherche sur Internet*. Montréal: CRÉPUQ, 1996. (En ligne) Adresse URL: http://www.bibl.ulaval.ca/vitrine/giri/giri2/

Mataigne, Bernard. *Internet à l'usage des pédagogues: une introduction*. (Note: Ce document se veut un outil aux mains des pédagogues (surtout du primaire et secondaire). Il se présente comme un instrument de premier niveau pour la découverte des possibilités éducatives d'Internet) (En ligne) Adresse URL: http://www.eduq.risq.net/DRD/P_telem/Internet.html

Resources in English

Australian Library and Information Association. School Libraries Section. *Information technology in schools: implications for teacher Librarians*. Perth : A.L.I.A., 1990. 92 p.

Barron, Ann; Ivers, Karen S. *The Internet and instruction: activities and ideas*. Englewood, CO: Libraries Unlimited, 1996.

The Canadian Teacher-Librarians' Resource Pages. (On line) URL address: http://Home.InfoRamp.Net/~abrown/

Clyde, Laurel A. *IASL, school libraries and the Internet*. 20 p. (Paper given at the XXVth annual conference, International Association of School librarianship, Ocho Rios, Jamaica, 1996.)

Clyde, Laurel A. "The Internet goes to school: use of the Internet in school libraries." In : *Online Information 94. 18th international online information meeting*. Proceedings. London, 6-8 December 1994. Edited by David I Raitt and Ben Jeapes. Oxford : Learned Information, 1994, pp. 233-242.

Clyde, Laurel A. *The school library as information provider : the home page. Discussion paper for the Second ITEC Virtual Conference "Schooling and the Networked World", April 1997*. (On line) URL address: http://www.rhi.hi.is/~anne/slhomepage.html

Garland, Kathleen; Scott, Sharon; Bayer, Kim. "Internet resources for professional information and support." *School library media annual*, vol. 13, 1995, pp. 233-246.

Harris, Judi. "Using Internet know-how to plan how students will know." *The Computing Teacher*, vol. 20, no 8, May 1993, pp 35-40.

Henri, James; Hay, Lyn. "T-Ls and the Internet: here come the cybarians!" *School libraries in Canada*, vol. 16, no 3, Summer 1996, pp. 19-20.

International Association of School Librarianship. *School Library resources on the Internet*. (On line). URL address: http://www.rhi.hi.is/~anne/linksiasl.html

Killan, Crawford. "Why teachers fear the Net." *Internet World*, november/December 1994, pp. 86-87.

140

Kuhlthau, Carol Collier (Ed.) *The virtual school library: gateway to the information superhighway.* M. Elspeth Goodin and Mary Jane McNally, associate editors. Englewood, CO: Libraries Unlimited, 1994. xi-152 p.

Kotlas, Carolyn (Comp.) *Evaluating web sites for educational uses : Bibliography and checklist Intitute for Academic Technology.* (On line) URL address: http://www.iat.unc.edu/guides/irg-49.html

Kurshan, Barbara L.; Wanamakera, Marcia A.; Millbury, Peter G. *Educator's guide to electronic networking: creating virtual communities.* Syracuse: Syracuse Univ., Information Resources Publications, 1994. 110 p.

McKenzie, Jamieson. "Beforenet and Afternet." *Multimedia Schools,* May/June, 1995.

Magid, Lawrence J. *Child Safety on the Information Highway.* Jointly produced by the National Center for Missing and Exploited Children and the Interactive Services Association. (On line) URL address: http://www.4j.lane.edu/InternetResources/Safety/Safety.html

Silva, Marcos. "The process of introducing Internet-based classroom projects and the role of school librarians." *Education for information,* vol. 13, no 3, 1995, pp. 243-252.

Valauskas, Edward J. "Education on-line: interactive K-12 computing." *On-line,* vol. 17, no 4, July 1993, pp. 89-91.

West, Peter. "The Mother of all networks." *Teacher magazine,* vol. 4, no 4, January 1993, pp. 19-22.

» QUELQUES SITES EN ÉDUCATION / A GLANCE AT SOME SITES IN EDUCATION

Ressources en français

Les bâtisseurs de l'inforoute : assistance et référence en conception de site Web au Québec. (Informations et liens vers d'autres ressources. Introduction à la création de documents pour le World Wide Web: guide élaboré par Oscar Figueiredo, École Polytechnique Fédérale de Lausanne) (En ligne) Adresse URL: http://diwww.epfl.ch/w3lsp/pub/coursweb/

Centre National de Documentation Pédagogique (France) (En ligne) Adresse URL: http://www.cndp.fr/

Ma région: un projet de télématique scolaire de la région Laval-Laurentides-Lanaudière qui relie 16 classes de quatrième année dans 11 commissions scolaires. (En ligne) Adresse URL: http://www.eduq.risq.net/DRD/P_telem/Gat_des.html

Le Réseau de télématique scolaire du Québec (RTSQ). (En ligne) Adresse URL: http://rtsq.grics.qc.ca/

Réseau scolaire canadien (En ligne) Adresse URL: http://www.rescol.ca/

Resources in English

AskERIC Service for Educators. (On line) Adresse URL: http://ericir.syr.edu/

Canada's SchoolNet. (On line) Adresse URL: http://www.schoolnet.ca/

EDTEC 572. Course about designing and delivering instructor-led lessons and workshops that are enhanced by technology, especially intranets and the Internet. (On line) URL address: http://edweb.sdsu.edu/courses/EDTEC572/edtec572.html

The Educational Resources Information Center (ERIC) (On line) URL address: http://www.aspensys.com/eric/index.html

International WWW Schools Registry. (On line) Adresse URL: http://web66.coled.umn.edu/schools.html

Landcare Education (Australia). Information or projects that may be useful for landcare education at primary or secondary school level. (On line) URL address: http://www.agfor.unimelb.edu.au/LCweb/lclibrary/edulcare.html

Librarians Information Online Network (LION). Sponsored by Library Services of the School District of Philadelphia as an information resource for school librarians in Philadelphia and throughout the nation. (On line) URL address: http://www.libertynet.org/~lion/lion.html

Media Awareness Network. For Educators is a clearinghouse of ideas, from educators to educators. It offers teaching units, student handouts, timely reports and background material for media education across the curriculum, K - 12. (On line) URL address: http://www.screen.com/mnet/eng/med/class/default.html

OZ_TEACHER NET. (Australia) Teachers helping teachers. A starting point for teachers who want to use the Internet for professional development and curriculum purposes. Maintained by Lindy Mc Keown. (On line) URL address: http://owl.qut.edu.au/oz-teachernet/

Silva, Marcos; Breuleux,Alain. "Canadian K-12 Networks: Issues and Models." *Electronic Journal on Virtual Culture,* vol. 3, no 3, August 31, 1995. (On line) URL address: http://www.marshall.edu/~stepp/vri/ejvc/ejvc.html

The Virtual Classroom: Artic Circle. (On line) URL address: http://www.lib.uconn.edu/ArcticCircle/VirtualClassroom/index.html

PROSPECTIVE

Des ressources rassemblées dans cet ouvrage il ressort que les bibliothèques et centres documentaires scolaires ont le vent dans les voiles, malgré des courants locaux quelquefois contraires... De plus, l'implantation et le développement des technologies de l'information en éducation renforce cette tendance, bien qu'il convienne d'être attentif à ne pas confondre la fin et les moyens.

Il s'agit, en fait, d'un changement de perspective portant non pas sur la nature imprimée ou électronique des supports, mais bien plutôt sur la façon d'utiliser les ressources en relation avec les objectifs des programmes d'études, qu'il s'agisse de fiction ou de documentation et que ces dernières soient disponibles localement ou accessibles à distance.

Durant la dernière décennie, les bibliothèques et centres documentaires scolaires ont connu des évolutions et des changements majeurs dans beaucoup de pays, lesquels se reflètent, entre autres, dans une terminologie variée: bibliothèque scolaire et centre ou service des média, centre d'apprentissage ou de ressources ou de connaissance, centre de documentation et d'information, etc. Dans certains pays, les bibliothèques et centres documentaires en milieu scolaire sont objet d'attention alors que, dans d'autres, elles affrontent des coupures budgétaires généralisées, une tendance à la gestion dé-centralisée voire, souvent, un manque d'intérêt.

Les bibliothécaires ou spécialistes de l'information ou enseignants-documentalistes en milieu scolaire vivent un défi continuel, face particulièrement à la rapide expansion des technologies, au besoin généralisé de développer la culture de l'information et aux bénéfices globaux susceptibles d'être retirés des apprentissages et de l'enseignement dits "basés sur les ressources".

C'est pour mieux refléter ce contexte global que la section des bibliothèques scolaires de l'IFLA vient de modifier son nom après 20 ans d'existence et qu'elle entend continuer à déployer ses efforts et faire entendre sa voix pour la promotion de la bibliothéconomie scolaire à travers le monde.

Je tiens à conclure cet ouvrage par un choix de citations que vous trouverez dans les pages qui suivent: mieux que ne pourrait le faire le discours d'une seule personne, elles illustrent collectivement les multiples dimensions des bibliothèques et des centres documentaires en milieu scolaire et le rôle des personnes qui en sont responsables.

Paulette Bernhard, Présidente, Section des bibliothèques et centres documentaires scolaires

From the resources collected in this book comes the evidence that school libraries and resource centers are sailing in favorable winds, even though they may encounter some adverse local currents... And the implementation and developement of information technologies in education strengthens this tendency, although one should seek not to confuse means and ends.

In fact, we face a change of perspective, concerned not so much with the printed or electronic nature of records, but more with the way these resources are used and integrated into the objectives of the curriculum, be they fiction or documentation, locally available or accessible through a network.

In the last decade, school libraries have been evolving and changing dramatically in many countries, which is reflected in the diversity of names: school library media service or center, learning or resource or knowledge center, documentation and information center, etc. School libraries seem to get attention and to be developing in some countries, while they face generalized budget cuts, a tendency toward local management and, often, a lack of recognition in others.

This is a challenging time for school librarians or teacher-librarians or information specialists, especially with the extraordinarily quick development of information technologies, the widespread need for develo-ping information literacy and the global benefits of resource-based learning and teaching.

It is in order to reflect this broad context that the Section of School Libraries has adopted a new name after 20 years of existence and keeps adding its voice and efforts for the promotion of school librarianship worldwide.

I do want to conclude this book with a selection of citations that you will find in the following pages: better than a one-person statement, they illustrate collectively the multiple dimensions of school libraries and resource centers and of those responsible for them.

Paulette Bernhard, Chair of the Section of School Libraries and Resource Centers

UN CHOIX DE CITATIONS / A SELECTION OF CITATIONS

À PROPOS DU CHANGEMENT EN ÉDUCATION / ABOUT CHANGE IN EDUCATION

"Education is changing from the assembly-line environment of the Industrial Age offered by textbook teaching to the data-rich environment of the information age offered by resource-based learning. In response to this change, the media center becomes the information center of the school, providing access to a wide range of resources and guidance in the process of learning from them." (Kuhlthau, 1989, p. 19)

"One curricular trend that will continue is the emphasis on pupils learning to learn, including their ability to handle and use information effectively. Given that pupils are likely to have increasingly large amounts of information available to them, the ability of the individual pupil to select relevant information will be crucial. (...) The quality of learning for pupils will depend not on the quantity on information available to them, but in the quality and relevance of the information, the appropriateness of the formats used, the level and style of language and images used, as well as the pupils' confidence and ability to select and use effectively the relevant information from that available. " (Herring, 1992, p. 133)

À PROPOS DU RÔLE DES BIBLIOTHÈQUES ET DES CENTRES DOCUMENTAIRES SCOLAIRES
ABOUT ROLE OF SCHOOL LIBRARIES AND RESOURCE CENTERS

"When a school is committed to establishing an environment that will encourage students to become learners all their lives, the school provides a school library media center whose programs take advantage of the enthusiasm of young people, teachers, and school library media center personnel for learning. This enthusiasm for learning is expressed through a sharing of knowledge and relevant materials. It is essential that school library media center programs be initiated in primary schools: to nurture the enthusiasm and enjoyment of learning and to establish early the concept of information seeking and handling." (Carroll, 1990, p. 5)

"Resource based learning implies active learning and should provide a means by which teachers are able to tailor learning resources, learning activities, the location of those activities, and learning expectations to the needs and abilities of each child. In order to maximize the achievement of learning outcomes, the teacher must establish learning objectives for each unit of work and adapt these to individual needs." (Henri, 1988, p. 7)

"At each independent school, a school library shall be established as a pedagogic service centre. The school library shall make teaching materials available for the teaching of the school, and it shall offer guidance in the use here of. The school library, moreover, contributes to promoting the school,s development by communicating relevant information." (Denmark. Ministry of Education. Regulations on school libraries [1993], p. 14)

À PROPOS DU RÔLE DU BIBLIOTHÉCAIRE ET DE L'ENSEIGNANT-DOCUMENTALISTE EN MILIEU SCOLAIRE / ABOUT THE ROLE OF SCHOOL- AND TEACHER-LIBRARIANS

" In spite of existing variations it is possible to identify three general knowledge factors which are essential for school librarians to be able to develop and operate effective school library programmes, i.e., information and library studies, management and instruction. Information and library studies is an essential component for the selection, organization and utilization of society's recorded information and ideas; Management involves the responsibility for the administration and daily operations of the school library and its personnel; Instruction signifies the interface with the classroom teachers in their instructional roles to develop effective information users." (Hannesdottir, 1995, p. 11)

À PROPOS DE L'APPRENTISSAGE DE LA LECTURE / ABOUT LEARNING TO READ

"Analyses of schools that have been successful in promoting independent reading suggest that one of the keys is ready access to books." (U.S. Commission on reading, 1985, p. 78)

À PROPOS DE LA CULTURE DE L'INFORMATION / ABOUT INFORMATION LITERACY

"Information seeking is a lifelong process, and skills for finding and using information must be extended throughout our formal and informal learning experiences. (...) "To learn how to select sources and how to address the various source options available may require training early in one's school career, on a generalized level." (Meadow, Marchionini, Cherry, 1994, p. 15)

"Notre action de formation doit donc conduire l'élève à construire à la fois des compétences techniques et informatives afin qu'il puisse intégrer le multimédia dans ses stratégies de recherche documentaire. (...) L'enjeu est de taille, car il s'agit de dépasser l'initiation technicienne et de conduire l'élève à construire de nouvelles compétences cognitives à travers la formation à la recherche multimédia." (Alava, 1994, p. 64)

À PROPOS DES TECHNOLOGIES DE L'INFORMATION / ABOUT INFORMATION TECHNOLOGIES

"But - no matter how large the Internet has become, nor how many gigabytes of data it holds - it still offers us only a glimpse of the services that will be possible in the future over truly broadband networks. It is a mistake to think that the Internet equals 'the information superhighway' for, with the exception of SuperJANET in the UK, we simply do not yet have a fully operational open broadband network for education. But what we do have, for those with the right equipment and connectivity, is the global Internet running over narrowband and linking over 30,000 smaller computer networks all over the world. At the time of writing, over 30 million people use it to exchange messages, obtain information about every subject imaginable and to take part in discussion groups. Highways for Learning is a basic introduction for teachers, trainers, lecturers and managers to an enormous subject and, while there are some technical details, the overall emphasis is on how the Internet might be used in education." (Great Britain. National Council for Educational Technology, On line 1996)

"Contrairement à la croyance populaire, l'adoption des technologies ne garantit pas de meilleurs résultats chez les élèves. De nombreux facteurs, et notamment la façon dont la technologie est mise en oeuvre et utilisée, jouent un rôle crucial dans l'obtention de ces résultats." (Industrie Canada, 1994, p. 70)

"Présentement, tous les milieux de travail sont à divers degrés pris dans ce tourbillon informationnel soulevé par les NTI. (...) Parallèlement, il n'y a pas une facette de notre profession qui ne soit pas aussi remodelée par ces technologies. C'est donc dire que notre profession se situe dans l'oeil même de l'ouragan informationnel." (Simoneau, 1995, p. 36)

À PROPOS DE L'UTILISATION DES TECHNOLOGIES PAR LES BIBLIOTHÉCAIRES ET ENSEIGNANTS-DOCUMENTALISTES EN MILIEU SCOLAIRE / ABOUT THE USE OF INFORMATION TECHNOLOGIES BY SCHOOL- AND TEACHER- LIBRARIANS

"This virtual conference experience for teacher librarians worldwide was a new and exciting way to communicate with international colleagues within a more structured, formal electronic forum, than the professional listservs of the Internet, which for many of us has become our daily professional lifeline through which we can tap into the collective wisdom of the profession." (Hay, Henri, 1996, p. i)

From 1993/1994 onwards, some schools (or classes within schools) began to develop World Wide Web sites. (...) It should be recognised from the beginning that the creation of a home page is not a "once only" activity. It is rather the beginning of an ongoing process that lasts as long as the home page is available for public viewing. The page will need to be maintained and updated regularly, again perhaps as a cooperative venture involving students and teachers, and within the context of information skills work. Links to other pages will have to be checked regularly to make sure that they are still active, and the information about the library kept up to date. New links and new content will be needed to keep the page interesting and relevant to the needs of users. Thus when resources (personnel, time, money, equipment) are allocated to this task, it should be on an ongoing basis. In addition, if a Web page is being developed as part of the school's educational programme, then students need to understand that these ongoing tasks are part of the process; through the ongoing maintenance of a Web page they gain a greater understanding of the volatile nature of the Internet. (Clyde, 1997, On line)

"Le documentaliste participe avec les autres enseignants à la formation ds individus, et sa connaissance des logiciels documentaires et du monde de la communication lui permet d'apporter sa contribution spécifique à cette formation. Aujourd'hui, encore bien plus qu'hier, il a la mission d'aider l'élève à être autonome dans la recherche d'information quel que soit le lieu où il se trouve, et quelle que soit la source qu'il interroge." (Morizio, Saj, Souchaud, 1996, p. 168)

À PROPOS DE LA RÉUSSITE EN RELATION AVEC DES BIBLIOTHÈQUES ET CENTRES DE RESSOURCES ADÉQUATEMENT ÉQUIPÉS ET DOTÉS EN PERSONNEL / ABOUT SUCCESS RELATED TO WELL EQUIPED AND STAFFED SCHOOL LIBRARIES AND RESOURCE CENTERS

"Si lire influence les résultats scolaires, aimer lire beaucoup est encore plus déterminant." (Québec. Ministère de l'Éducation, 1994, p. 40)

148

"When we combine the Colorado study and the Krashen review of research, a powerful model appears that can become the basis of a solid reading program for schools. (...) Simply put, adequate SLMC budgets, materials, and staffing, as well as techniques that encourage the effective use of library resources, lead to higher student achievement." (Loertscher, 1993, p. 33)

"Students in schools with well-equipped resource centers and professional teacher-librarians will perform better on achievement tests for reading comprehension and basic research skills." (Haycock,1992, p. 13)

SOURCES

Alava, Séraphin. "Naviguer sans se noyer : multimédia et médiation documentaire." *Inter-CDI*, no 132, nov.-déc, 1994, pp. 64-68.

Carroll, Frances Laverne. *Guidelines for school libraries.* The Hague: IFLA, 1990. 40 p. (IFLA professional reports; 20)

Clyde, Laurel A. *The school library as information provider : the home page. Discussion paper for the Second ITEC Virtual Conference "Schooling and the Networked World",* April 1997. (On line) URL address: http://www.rhi.hi.is/~anne/slhomepage.html

Denmark. Ministry of Education. Regulations on school libraries (1993). In: Danish Association of School Librarians; Danish Association of School Libraries *School libraries in Denmark.* By Hanne Heiselberg, Niels Jacobsen and Inga Nielsen. Viby Zealand: The Danish Association of School Librarians, 1997, pp. 14-15.

Great Britain. National Council for Educational Technology . *Highways for learning: an introduction to the Internet for schools and colleges.* 1995. (On line, 1996) URL address: http://www.ncet.org.uk/publications/highways/

Hannesdottir, Sigrun Klara. *School librarians: guidelines for competency requirements.* The Hague: IFLA, 1995. 46 p. (IFLA professional reports; no 41)

Hay, Lyn; Henri, James (Eds.). *A meeting of the minds: ITEC virtual conference '96 proceedings.* (Perth): Australian School Library Association, 1996. 232 p.

Haycock, Ken. *What works: research about teaching and learning through the school's library resource center.* Seattle, WA; Vancouver: Rockland Press, 1992. 230 p.

Henri, James. *The school curriculum: a collaborative approach to learning.* 2nd ed. Wagga Wagga, NSW: Charles Sturt University, Centre for Library Studies, 1988. 140 p.

Herring, James. *Information technology in schools: the role of the school librarian and the teacher.* 2nd ed. of The microcomputer, the school librarian and the teacher. London: Library Association Publishing, 1992. viii-150 p.

Industrie Canada. Direction du développement des communications. *Les possibilités éducatives de l'autoroute de l'information au Canada : utilisation et instauration des technologies de l'information et communications en éducation.* Par Luc Fournier et Kim MacKinnon. Ottawa : octobre 1994. viii, 102 p. + annexes.

Kuhkthau, Carol C. " Information search process: a summary of research and implications for school libray media programs." *School library media quarterly,* vol. 18, no 1, 1989, pp. 19-25.

Loertscher, David V. "*Objective:* achievement. *Solution:* School libraries." *School library journal,* vol. 39, May 1993, pp. 30-33.

Meadow, Ch. T.; Marchionini, G.; Cherry, J.M. "Speculations on the measurement and use of user characteristics in information retrieval experimentation." *Revue canadienne des sciences de l'information et de bibliothéconomie,* vol. 19, no 4, 1994, pp. 1-22.

Morizio, Claude; Saj, Marie-Paule; Souchaud, Michel. *Les technologies de l'information au CDI.* Paris: Hachette Éducation, 1996. 190 p.

Québec. Ministère de l'Éducation. Direction de la recherche. *Compétences et pratiques de lecture des élèves québécois et français : une comparaison Québec-France.* [Recherche et analyse : Guy Legault; Lise Giroux.] Québec : le ministère, juin 1994. 39 p.

Simoneau, Marcel. "La reconnaissance de l'acte professionnel: pour la valorisation de notre savoir-faire dans l'organisation." *Argus,* vol. 24, no 1, janvier-avril 1995, pp. 36-38.

U.S. Commission on reading. *Becoming a nation of readers.* The report of the Commission... Prepared by Richard C. Anderson, Richard C., Elfrieda H. Hiebert, Judith A. Scott, Ian A.G. Wilkinson. Washington, D.C. : The National Academy of Reading, 1985.